# *The Reluctant Bride*

A NOVEL

C. K. Veale

This book is a work of fiction. Places, events, and situations in this story are purely fictional. Any resemblance to actual persons, living or dead, is coincidental.

© 2001, 2002, 2003 by C. K. Veale. All rights reserved.

No part of this book may be reproduced, stored in a retrieval system, or transmitted by any means, electronic, mechanical, photocopying, recording, or otherwise, without written permission from the author.

ISBN: 1-4107-0066-6 (e-book)
ISBN: 1-4107-0067-4 (Paperback)

Library of Congress Control Number: 2002096327

This book is printed on acid free paper.

Printed in the United States of America
Bloomington, IN

1stBooks - rev. 10/29/03

*for C.A.S.A.*

*and*

*The Children*

# *Prologue*

Julia's disappearance ended in a dark, airless room two thousand miles south of the border with a proclamation delivered by an old Mexican woman—a psychic named La Señora—who sat hunched over a glass ball, murmuring to herself in Spanish. Julia stared in shocked silence at the ball, as La Señora, the mouthpiece of celestial wisdom, revealed the latest twist in the plot of Julia's life.

"Can you double check?" Julia asked hopefully. She had a right to ask. After all, she had just been informed, in no uncertain terms, that within a matter of months her life would be drastically and forever changed.

"No checks. You *will* marry." To Julia these words were not cookies on a plate to be graciously accepted or declined, they were tablets of stone. La Señora was the one person Julia trusted with her future, for she had been dead-on accurate in the past and Julia was convinced that the gray-haired Mexican woman could decipher all the lines on the palm of Fate. That didn't stop Julia, however, from trying to talk her out of it.

"You're kidding, right?" she asked, breaking into a cold sweat. "This is not at all what I had in mind for myself. It doesn't fit with my plan," she explained. She held her hands out to La Señora, fingers splayed to support the load of her imaginary plan.

La Señora stared at Julia's empty palms. "Plan? What plan, Julia (who-lee-uh)?" The old woman dabbed at her face with an embroidered handkerchief. This prompted Julia to raise the back of her hand to test her own forehead. It was hot and moist—a fever maybe. She had no actual plan, nothing more than what she'd been doing for the last two years since her husband Turner's death—running.

"No, Julia," she said wagging an arthritic finger at her, "Is true." She had that written-in-cement look on her face. Julia had seen that look before and knew there would be no concessions. La Señora was certain, as certain as a summer day in Mexico is long, hot and sticky. Julia turned her face up to the ceiling fan for reprieve from the heat, to collect her thoughts, to find a way out. As if to emphasize the futility of escape, the fan chose that very moment to stop working, the blades slowing to stillness as the small room in which the two women sat began to surrender to the heat of the day. Julia stared at the blades of the traitorous fan until it was motionless and her neck ached. It was at that moment Julia felt the full weight of La Señora's prediction and understood that the Fates had intervened once again in her life. Like it or not she would be getting married some time this year. It was a done deal.

"But I don't want to get married," she enunciated each syllable clearly, slowly, as she leaned across the rickety cardtable that separated them, a pained look on her face. La Señora sat back, folded her arms across the shelf of her bosom, lifted her left eyebrow into an unnatural peak and nodded at the ball that sat in the middle of a twelve-inch square of burgundy felt, as if to say, "How can you argue with that?"

Julia directed her attention and disbelief to the ball. It was, in fact, a glass snow-scene ball, the kind children receive at Christmas. When she was a child, balls such as this had to be turned upside down, then righted for the snow to fall on the pastoral scene within, but now advanced technology insured a perpetual mini blizzard independent of operator intervention. She glared at the snow that whipped around the two fair-haired ceramic children who resided within, arms lifted in obvious wonder and delight. La Señora reached across the table and laid a consoling hand on Julia's knee. "*Tenga confianza en la vida,*" she instructed. Trust. Have faith in life.

In spite of everything, Julia did trust life—always had. She suddenly remembered a conversation some years past, when La Señora had confided that she didn't really need the ball, the benefit being strictly for her clients. "It calms them to watch the snow," La Señora had said. The memory made Julia laugh at herself and the absurdity of sitting in a tiny, sweltering room in Manzanillo, glaring accusingly at the artificial telltale snowflakes. Her own reflection and that of the room was superimposed on the convexity of the glass ball. Had she brought her Nikon, she would have photographed the dual image she saw, children playing in a ceaseless swirl of white—her future held in snowflakes—momentarily captured by the dark closeness of the humid room. As she leaned in closer, looking for clues, her reflected image spread across the parabola of the glass. Her eyes looked huge in this distorted view, appropriately so, for they held her past.

Behind Julia, the curtain that separated the two women from the brightness of the day fluttered just enough to be noticed in the reflection of the ball. Plaid, frayed at the bottom and tacked randomly at the top it had hung, stirred by the occasional breeze, year after year, faded by the sun that pushed against it and soiled by the candied hands of children riding past on their bicycles. Only this cotton curtain separated the mundane from the future, as predicted by a seventy-year-old Mexican woman.

La Señora covered the glass ball with both hands and locked eyes with Julia, "Like before, it is true," she said. The two women looked deeply into one another's eyes, silently acknowledging their roles in this new drama about to unfold.

It had been five years since La Señora had predicted Turner's appearance and importance in her life. "Are you this accurate with everyone?" Julia had asked. In response, La Señora had provided her with a thumbnail sketch on the subtle art of snowball interpretation. She explained that she received only general information for the majority of those seeking her services, but was somehow provided specific and detailed visions for a chosen few. She was an antenna, of sorts, for the ones to whom she had been assigned. Julia had been one of these.

La Señora considered the guidance of her clients as her true purpose in life and was deeply offended by anything less than whole-hearted acceptance of her pronouncements. Julia also knew that La Señora would not let her out of the room until she acknowledged the fact she was indeed going to be married sometime this year.

"Okay, Señora, I understand," she said, with as much enthusiasm as she could muster. She reached for her purse.

La Señora waved away her offer to pay. Julia glanced around the room at the assortment of 8X10 glossies tacked to the wall that she had provided in payment for other sessions. "Photo?"

"*Sí. Foto. Por favor.*"

La Señora was a psychic who never seemed to grow tired of her own likeness. At first Julia thought it simple vanity, but as she had come to know her better, she'd seen something more in the psychic's infatuation with her own image. It was La Señora's way of holding on to the physical world, an essential exercise for those who straddle both realms. Julia had her own way of grounding herself and, since Turner's death, she'd often used it to make sense of the few short years they'd had together. She sat naked, cross-legged in front of a full-length mirror and, staring deeply into her own eyes, asked the middle-aged woman who stared back at her, "Who are you? Aren't you done yet?"

Knowing she'd learn nothing more from La Señora that day, Julia made her way to the curtained exit. "Thank you," she said, glancing back over her shoulder. She tried to be grateful for any guidance that came her way. Whenever the spirit world decided to offer up a signpost, the least she could do was pay attention.

* * *

**She pushed back the curtain** and stepped into the bright heat of the afternoon. It was just past siesta and the streets were beginning to fill with people, some on their way back to work, others heading toward the beach where they would finish their afternoon in the shade of a *palapa.* A young man in a maroon shirt and a black cowboy hat leaned against a bright blue wall and played a guitar made of highly polished wood the color of autumn. The tune he played was melancholy and difficult enough to demand his full attention. He didn't notice Julia. He didn't see her leave La Señora's. He didn't see his song enter her, comfort her and move her across the street toward him, then past. His melody accompanied her two blocks down *Avenida del Sueños* and, although she could barely see the guitarist as she entered *Casa de Bob*, she could still hear his tune—or so she imagined.

"Julia! *Hola Amiga*!"

She was snapped out of her ruminations momentarily by Juanda, a curly-haired Mexican flamer who rushed toward her, arms flapping. His eye makeup was thick; his eyebrows sculpted into dark bird wings. *Probably drawn on with magic markers.* "Kiss, Kiss," he said to both of her cheeks.

He hooked her arm in his and walked her over to a seaside table, conspiratorially whispering the day's fare, as if the other patrons weren't privy to the whims of Chef Bob. An old red and blue Cinzano umbrella managed to shade only a quarter of the table where he seated her. He stepped back, critically assessed the situation, spun the umbrella a half turn to add another inch or two of shade to the table and with a '*voila*' hand gesture deemed it adequate, explaining that the sun was shifting and more shade would be arriving shortly.

She took the seat he flamboyantly offered and after exchanging the requisite pleasantries, eagerly scanned the bright, slick menu he laid with a flourish in front of her to see what new fare they had managed to concoct. Bob and Juanda were going for a new image this season, something with a European flair. They'd had the menu translated to English for the Canadian and American tourists who would flood the port town once December's cold reached the northern continent. As usual, the translation didn't quite hit its mark. The new menu boasted savory items such as *Head Liver to the Raisins of Grapes, Fillit Tips to the Garlic* and *Skewer of Shrimp Niza Racetrack.* A small complementary plate of *ceviche*, chips and a bowl of *limones* appeared on the table as Julia decided to try the *Hot Foot of Frog Legs to the Kitchen of Barcelona.* One could only imagine. Always on the lookout for adventure, she boldly ordered.

Four o'clock in the afternoon and still too hot. *Time to move on.* The heat slid across the top layer of sand. She squinted until the undulating waves of heat took on a mirage effect. She always hoped to see some miraculous twist of sight on days like today. Some

Mexican angel perhaps, materializing there, just there, by the volleyball net, or perhaps a vision of her next husband wandering along the tide line. Instead, she saw a young, well-built woman with long dark hair, sprint across the hot sand to the water's edge and plunk herself down unceremoniously in the wet sand. Nothing seemed out of the ordinary. Down the beach a boy pushed an umbrellaed *Raspas* hand truck. Children's outstretched hands begged *pesos* from their parents as he approached with his icy treats. *I don't need a husband. I don't want one.* She had nothing against men, liked them a lot actually, sometimes too much. And as for marriage, there were aspects she truly enjoyed. She'd grown to cherish cuddling next to the warmth and safety of Turner at night and missed it still. But marriage? It just asked too much of a woman, at least a woman like herself.

She squeezed more *limone* on her *ceviche* while she thought over La Señora's prediction. She looked up to see a young couple arrive with a small child, a girl, all pink and frilled. They ordered two cokes as they came through the restaurant and sat down at the table next to Julia. The little girl flirted with Juanda while her parents bent, foreheads furled, over the unfamiliar menu and its cryptic fare.

Having children was one adventure the fates had spared her, and was possibly her only regret. But she knew the life she had led would not have been possible with children. A child would have changed her. If she'd had a child she would have cluttered its life with lessons, teachers, excursions and all the other things she had not been given when she was young. She had reconciled herself to childlessness long ago, but there were mornings, even after the hysterectomy, when she would wake up and for some unexplainable reason think, *maybe I'm pregnant.*

* * *

**By now it was clear** life would have its way with her. She had to accept the fact. *So, I guess I'll be getting married this year.* She laughed out loud at the thought. The couple next to her smiled and looked with pride at their daughter—assuming her laughter had been prompted by their wonderful offspring—while Julia, accepting La Señora's declaration, paged through her notebook for a clean sheet and began writing an invitation to her wedding. "The pleasure of your company is requested at my wedding on . . ." She looked at her watch, ". . . December 31, 2002." *Might as well give myself as much time as possible to find this wonderful new guy.*

"What are you writing?" Juanda inquired as he leaned over her shoulder to refill her water glass.

"My wedding invitation," she declared flatly.

"Julia!" arms waving, "*A quien*?" (To whom?)

"Oh, I don't know," she replied and tossed him a sideways, mischievous grin.

"Me, Julia! Make it me!" he begged, dropping to one knee. Julia laughed and kissed his forehead.

"Not a chance. Then I'd have to marry Bob, too, and what would I do with two husbands?"

He looked around as if to insure that no one was listening, "We could be very good to you, Julia," he said softly, slowly, in his best Errol Flynn imitation, giving her thigh a possessive pat. Meaning, in fact, that her money could be very good for the two of them.

For an instant she considered the offer. Great meals, lots of laughs, and then . . .

"Juanda, I'm afraid I'm just not *that* adventurous."

"Okay," he replied with feigned disappointment. He rose, brushing imaginary insults off his imaginary lapels, tossed his head in the air and, with a dramatic downward gaze, said "You DON'T know what you're missing," before seductively strolling off.

What she would be missing, and soon, were the friends and this cast of characters who colored the village she had hoped she could call home. Her life was an ex-patriot's dream, but she felt the pull of her family and friends in California gaining momentum, like a wave that uses the rip tide to gather strength before it crests.

A bird landed apprehensively on the back of the chair across from her. The baby at the next table went crazy with delight. "*Pajarito,*" the parents said, pointing to the bird. "Bird," Julia, always the teacher, said in the direction of the baby. The parents smiled and nodded their approval. The baby was about to tumble out of her seat as she strained to get at the bird. Her squeals didn't detour the bird from hopping onto the table in search of the random tortilla chip. *What it must be like to see the world through the eyes of a child. What it must be like to be a child.* Julia's heart swelled.

After Turner died, she'd begun to carry a notebook to jot down random thoughts in an attempt to sort through her pain and guilt. Lately, however, her memories had turned more and more to her younger sister, Shelly.

The baby at the next table shrieked something that sounded like "Yikes!" and flung a tortilla chip at the bird. Julia flipped a page in her notebook and began to write:

*We were, both of us in her turn, robbed of our childhoods. It was sucked out of us smoothly, effortlessly, like the meat of a shelled oyster, swallowed up in one easy motion, leaving behind the shell, its iridescence vulnerable and exposed, with nothing to latch onto. No center, no core, and certainly no pearl.*

*We watched other children playing carefree. When their playtime concluded, we saw them run to their mothers and walk off hand-in-hand, chatting and skipping by their sides. We watched a father's hand smooth the hair on the beloved head that rested in his arms. Because of her tucked-in, storytime nights, we knew her dreams would be sweeter than ours.*

*I guess you could say there were advantages. The dangers lurking in the dark didn't frighten us compared to what we endured in daylight hours. And if some boogeyman beneath our beds wanted to crawl out and snatch us away in the night, so be it. Maybe life was better in boogeyville.*

*Shelly, in her childish attempt to deal with her daily ration of cruelty, tried her best to melt seamlessly into the kitchen walls. She couldn't quite disappear, but she did manage to grow flatter and flatter as the years went by. She is forever stalked by nameless fears and faceless terrors. A part of her remains to this day, caught in the carousel wallpaper above the kitchen table. The house is still there; nothing much has changed. If you visit, and look closely, you can see her there, eyes wide, her mouth in a perpetual 'O' of protestation. Look for a child atop a raging black plastic horse, endlessly circling what might have been her life.*

# *Paula:*

The invitation came in the mail ten days ago. I recognized her handwriting immediately—bold, flourished and uneven, at times slanting upward, at times down. Just like Julia herself. A no-brainer for a handwriting analyst. "*The pleasure of your company is requested at my wedding which is to be held at Schoolhouse Beach, Bodega, California, at 6 p.m., December 31, 2002. Dress: Casual.*" The name of her Intended a glaring omission.

In that Julia's wedding was only three months away, I did what any woman would do. I went straight to my closet. Pushing aside my work clothes, the jackets, suits and blouses I hoped to find something, anything, suitable for such an occasion. I was looking for something that would suggest casual-elegance; something one would wear to her best friend's wedding on a windswept Northern California beach at sunset in the middle of winter. It would be tough to achieve the right look beneath a fleece-lined parka. Well, there was no help for it. Time for a new outfit. *What the hell is she doing?!*

As I feverishly pawed through my closet, dismissing Armani and torturing my best silks, I realized my anger was only distracting me from my true feelings. She'd been my best friend since our college days and I felt hurt and left out. I had no idea she's been planning to marry again, not to mention she's been missing-in-action for the last two years and we've had no obligatory chats over the obvious merits and potential flaws of her future husband. In fact, all I'd received over the course of her disappearance were generic little notes about this place or that—whatever would fit on the back of a postcard. Totally unsatisfactory and not good best-friend etiquette.

Downstairs I poured myself a cup of decaf from my ever-faithful Mr. Coffee, the one appliance that hadn't broken down recently. I snatched an almond biscotti from my stash of emergency sweets and shuffled into the living room. "Cookie?" a familiar squawk beckoned. I broke off a Hartz Mountain-size piece for Polo, my African Gray, a totally useless pet and constant reminder of a rocky two-year relationship with Todd, my ex-boyfriend and manager of the Feathered Friends Pet Shop. Our relationship ended one rainy night when he insisted Polo sleep with us. In the middle of a fabulous dream featuring Harrison Ford in his sexiest roll, I half-awoke to find Polo kneading my chest, beak open. I jumped up, screeched a few choice obscenities and flung him half way across the room. Todd naturally ran to Polo's rescue, cooing and baby talking him out of the corner. When he finally looked my way I knew it was over. His pinched face made it clear he would forevermore see me as a bird abuser. A nasty fight ensued, our differences becoming more apparent with each verbal blow. Polo, thankfully, sided with me, sitting on my shoulder and offering what seemed at the moment to be perfectly-timed squawks. More to prove a point than for actual affection for Polo I insisted the bird stay with me. He was, after all, a birthday gift and familiar with his surroundings. I didn't have to say he'd seen the last of my bedroom. It was understood. Just as it was understood that Todd shared the same fate, as I handed him his backpack and ushered him out the front door at three in the morning.

I plunked myself down on the couch and with biscotti crumbs accumulating on my new Karen Newburger nightshirt, I surveyed my surroundings. The tasteful sleek elegance of the living room furniture contrasted beautifully against the tonal qualities of the glazed faux finish. Lynn Augstein, color guru of Sausalito, had mixed a sumptuous palette and gently crafted a space that was truly me. I couldn't wait to show it off. Problem was, I couldn't find a man as interesting as my living room.

* * *

**Saturday morning and I could sculpt the day** to my choosing. I could hike around Spring Lake, cycle the Dry Creek Valley, attend any number of wine tasting/jazzy events at the local wineries or take in a foreign flick at the Lakeside Cinema. Life in Sonoma Valley was never boring. So why did I feel limp? I strolled aimlessly through the house trying to discern the source of my discontent, focusing momentarily on the stack of journals I had yet to read. I had been known to pile up a year's worth of untouched

Psychology Today's and still feel jubilant, so I couldn't pin it on mounting guilt and trade publications. It hit me on my return trip to Mr. Coffee. Although the space I inhabit and call home is perfect, there's no one here but me. I reached into the cookie jar for a second biscotti—this time the hard stuff, Chocolate Almond Amaretto.

Here was Julia about to embark upon her fourth marriage and I'd not walked down the aisle once. Not even close. Not even as a bridesmaid. No one can understand why I'm still single. I'm an attractive, slim, well-adjusted professional. Never mind I'm on the verge of turning fifty, I've worked out nearly every day of my adult life and I look terrific. I eat well, sneaking sweets only under extreme stress, my teeth are good and the only signs of menopause are fitful sleep patterns and a lack of tolerance in certain situations. My moods have yet to start swinging and my memory is still intact. The upshot of all this? I consider myself a good catch. However, at the end of the day when I leave my office and jog the two blocks down Fourth Street to the parking garage I can almost hear the women of Santa Rosa—both young and matronly—whispering to each other: "*Thank God for her career.*" If it weren't for my practice people would think there's something fundamentally wrong with me. At least my credentials give them a reason why I haven't settled down. *She could have been happily married with children, but nooo, she had to pursue that career of hers.*

In all fairness, when it comes to love I have to admit I haven't always made the best choices. I seem to be attracted to men who are broken in some way. They need me and I know I can fix them. Or at least come close. It's an irresistible combination.

Julia, on the other hand, had always made good choices when it came to men. All three of her ex-husbands had been great guys. In each case her hasty decision to marry took everyone off guard, as she had always been headstrong, independent and completely ambivalent about marriage. I secretly suspected she had said yes to keep the guys from losing face. I guess she just decided to dive in and figured it would all work out somehow. Underlying everything, Julia loved change and marriage allowed her to turn another page in her life. Once married she seemed to enjoy herself. A little too much. Her world continued to swarm with great guys and Julia couldn't get clear on the concept of fidelity. In psych terms she had a hard time establishing boundaries for herself, and it had cost her.

"I'm a physical person," she explained to me one day during our downward-facing-dog pose at Yogurt & Yoga. "I like kissing and touching and making love. I really don't think God would judge me on that score. In fact, what could be more pleasing to God than loving others?" Her first two husbands hadn't seen it that way. Although Julia had been sad to see them go, it had never quite made sense to her. Why had they been such sticklers on the monogamy issue, when she had been a loving and devoted wife in all other regards?

By the time Turner came along she had changed her ways, explaining that nothing was worth the pain her infidelities had inflicted on those she loved. It had been a good thing too, because

Turner the Texan had preconceived notions of where his wife would be at all times, none of which included another man's bed.

Julia had been true to her word. And Turner, the persuasive businessman with his formidable i-dotting and t-crossing ways, had made sure their wedding vows left no room for interpretation. There were a lot of *always and forever* in that ceremony. Had he lived, I feel certain Julia would have kept her promise, after all he hadn't asked her to obey. She had drawn the line on that one.

My fingers trailed over the words of her announcement, hoping for some clue as to what was going on, wanting to be close like we once were. As usual, she had left no way to contact her and try as I might I wasn't picking up any vibes from the invitation. I set it down and walked over to the phone. Surely I wasn't the only one on Julia's guest list and if anyone knew more than me, it would be Shelly.

I poured myself another cup of coffee, walked to the phone, picked up the receiver, and put it down. Walked away. Sighed, walked back and started dialing.

"Lo!," came the response.

"Daryl?"

"Yeah, who's this?"

"It's Paula. Is Shelly there?"

"Yeah, but make it short. I'm expecting a call."

Over the years I had allowed myself the luxury of forgetting just how obnoxious Shelly's husband could be.

"OK?" he demanded.

"OK, Daryl, I can hear you just fine. Your phone is operational. No need to shout."

"Shell, it's Paula," he yelled, adding another dimension of volume to the already noisy background. I could hear the TV blaring a feminine hygiene commercial while kids shrieked at one another: "Give it, Daimon. I'm telling Mom!"

More shrieks and pounding feet followed before Shelly finally picked up the phone.

"Sam, let him play with it til I get off the phone, then he'll give it back—OK, Daimon? (silence) OK with you, Sam?"

"Paula!" she said into the receiver, finally disengaged from the chaos. I imagined her grabbing a full ashtray and parking herself in a chair beside a kitchen sink overflowing with last night's dishes. Shelly had never been a great housekeeper and now with two kids under the age of six, I could guess what the house looked like on a Saturday morning. Little did I know I was soon to find out.

"Hi Shell."

"Paula, where have you been?"

"Right here in Santa Rosa. You know I have a practice over on Fourth Street, don't you?"

"Oh, right."

"Sorry I haven't been in touch. How are things?"

"Oh, you know, Daryl."

Unfortunately, I did. She had tried several times to get away from him, but could never quite make the break permanent. Before Julia left, she had worked hard getting Shelly set up in a place of her own. I was in the room the day Shelly told Julia she was returning home to Daryl. "It's the Christian thing to do, and I don't want to hear any more about inner voices and higher selves" she had explained to her big sister, "It's probably just the Devil anyway." Daryl had started going to some bible-thumping congregation and had pulled Shelly with him, convincing her that life would be different now that they were going to be Christians. Naturally he played up the forgiveness factor of their religion to make his screw-ups palatable.

Julia, not being overly fond of organized religion to begin with, saw through the ruse. Neither Shelly nor I had ever seen her lose her temper before, so we were both surprised when she hurled a bowl of Santa Rosa plums toward her, missing as intended, but causing a lot of noise and a big mess. "This is what your life is going to look like little Christian!" she yelled, glaring at Shelly. Then she proceeded to smush those plums into the kitchen floor with her new Reeboks.

"Anything new?" I fished. "Have you heard anything from Julia?" *She'll find out sooner or later anyway.*

"Just the usual. No, nothing really. Why?"

"The usual? What do you mean?"

"Well I haven't actually talked to her since she left two years ago, but . . ."

"But what?"

"Well, she calls every couple of months or so and leaves some Julia-like message."

"But you don't talk to her directly?"

"Paula. She evidently doesn't want to talk. She always calls in the middle of the night when the machine is on."

"And what sort of message does she leave?"

"Oh, you know. Something inspirational, like oh I don't know, focusing on the good and trusting the cosmos. Julia stuff."

"That's it?"

"Not exactly. Once Daimon had an ear infection, and I was up walking him around trying to get him back to sleep when she called. I picked up the phone."

"And? What did she say?"

"She said, 'Love you Shelly,' and hung up."

"Nothing else?"

"Nope. She hung up. There I was, standing barefoot in the kitchen, middle of the night with Daimon screaming his head off—he hates it when I talk on the phone. I had so much to tell her, Paula, and she didn't give me a chance. She hung up before I could even tell her I love her too."

Clearly she didn't know about the wedding and I didn't want to be the one to tell her, at least not while she was choking back tears.

"Paula, can I ask you a favor?"

"Sure."

"Can you come over?"

*I* couldn't not go. First, I owed it to Julia and second I am a therapist and this was obviously a cry for help. I bought myself a little time by promising to come over later in the day. She assured me that Daryl would be out of the house by two in the afternoon. That gave me my usual hour at the gym, plus a little time for the errands I had been putting off.

I concentrated on my breathing, the other people in the gym, anything to keep my mind off Shelly. I had twenty minutes to go on the treadmill. I couldn't fight it any longer. I let my memories stray onto the minefield of Shelly Collin's life. It was not a pleasant place although truth be told, my first encounter with Shelly, some thirty years ago, had sealed my fate as a therapist.

* * *

**I was a student at Sonoma State College**, getting my liberal art requirements out of the way before choosing between psychology and viticulture majors. Julia and I were roommates, sharing an old rundown farmhouse. It was during finals. Our study habits were similar, which is to say we both crammed long after more methodical students were asleep. We had just decided that we had put in sufficient time, closed the books, and discovering that we were too hopped up on NoDoz and Folgers to sleep, had settled into a late night movie when the phone rang. Nora's neighbor was frantic, claiming that Nora had gone crazy and was throwing buckets of water all over the house while swearing so loudly at Shelly she was waking half the neighborhood.

I insisted on accompanying Julia to the dingy little seaside town of Pacifica, a mere two-hour drive, to rescue her ten-year-old sister. I didn't know what to expect. Having grown up with two relatively normal parents in an affluent neighborhood in San Francisco where dinner was served promptly at five every evening, hadn't prepared me for Nora. Julia had expected to find her mother drunk, screaming and bouncing Shelly around the room like a racquetball. According to Julia, Nora was prone to this type of behavior whenever her world went sideways, which, it seemed, was often. Julia wanted to bring Shelly home with us. As she drove Julia rehearsed the argument she would use to persuade her mother to relinquish custody. I stared out into the black night trying hard to imagine sharing Julia and our cozy little life with an adolescent. I was less than thrilled at the prospect.

We were both prepared for a full-blown confrontation, so when we arrived to find Nora sitting silently at the kitchen table in her robe, chain smoking and drunk on cheap red wine, we weren't sure how to proceed, or what to say. The scent of fear seemed to comingle with the alcoholic stench and second-hand smoke that permeated the walls of the dark house. I realized instantly that I was way out of my depth and decided to merely stand by while Julia sorted it out.

Evidently an explanation for our sudden appearance at three in the morning was not required nor expected. Nora barely looked up from her wine glass. She seemed to be communing with it somehow, humming it a little song.

"Where's Shelly," Julia asked, pouring us both a glass of water. I felt invisible and was content to remain that way.

"Sleeping," came the reply. Nora's elbow rested on the table as she simultaneously supported her head and brought her cigarette to her lips with the same hand. Her other hand kept beat to some internal symphony which she tapped out on the kitchen table. The neighbor had described flood waters and we had discussed the necessity of bringing waders. That would have been a bit of overkill.

Although the house was somewhat dank, there were no lakes to be forged as I followed Julia into Shelly's room. She tried to wake her by gently shaking the lump in the bed. No response. She shook it harder. "Shelly, get up. We're going. You can't live like this anymore." A bearded face emerged from under the covers.

In the kitchen, the silent symphony played on. "Mom, there's a man in Shelly's bed. Do you know who he is? And where is Shelly?" Julia said leaning in toward her mother, enunciating clearly as if alcohol affected one's hearing. "Remember the fairytales, Mom?

Little children are supposed to be tucked safely in their beds at night."

"You are in my house, missy," Nora slurred, "Don't you use that tone on me. For your information that man is Ramon, my tenant, sound asleep in his rented room, at least until now. As if I need to explain anything to you!"

I doubted Ramon had slept through a commotion that awakened the neighbors, nor the insistent shaking by Julia, but I saw no need to point it out.

Julia brought her face level with her mother's and stared hard.

"She sleeps on the couch," Nora finally offered.

"So, Shelly's room is the couch. Figures." I followed Julia into the living room. Shelly was awake and had heard everything, yet she still lay silently in the darkness of the room. A street lamp cast a thin trail of light across the couch. It was filtered through gauzy yellowed curtains and outlined Shelly's slight, prepubescent form, curled up fetal style. My heart warmed and opened as I imagined what she must be feeling, thinking.

"Shelly, get up honey," Julia said. She leaned over to smooth the hair from Shelly's eyes. She was motionless, lying in a clump of blankets, eyes focused elsewhere, saying nothing.

"Shelly, please get up. I'm taking you to Santa Rosa to live with me and Paula," she tried brightly. I smiled and nodded my head in agreement with the plan, hoping to encourage some response. I wanted to leave and prayed Julia could motivate her sister quickly.

"No," barely audible, came the reply.

"What?"

"I'm not going."

"Why?" Julia asked. I wasn't sure what I expected, but I had assumed there would be a little more compliance on Shelly's part. *Maybe she's in shock.*

"Mom needs me."

"What are you talking about? Needs you for what?"

"The dust. The dust hurts her asthma. I have to keep the dust out of this house!" she explained through clenched teeth, talking as loudly as humanly possible while barely opening her mouth. Julia would later explain that Nora's asthma was bad, and regardless of how many inhalers she used or how many bottles of Prednisone she emptied, there was never quite enough air in her world for her to be at ease with her breathing.

"You don't have to do any such thing. Now get up. She'll manage without you."

Shelly sat up slowly, the street light skimming the edges of her white-blond hair, giving her an ethereal glow.

"No," she said, "I'm not going anywhere with YOU. You're evil. You're a devil worshiper."

Julia looked stunned. She sat down on the couch next to her sister and turned her chin until they were eye to eye. "Where did you ever get an idea like that?"

"Mom told me. She said I should never trust you. You're tinted."

"The word is *tainted*, and I am not." Even in the dark I could tell Julia was incensed.

She was not expecting this from a sister who loved her and whom she had loved and cared for all her life.

"We were having a seance, me and Mom and Ramon . . ."

Julia interrupted, "What? You're having seances now?"

". . . and Mom felt an evil presence and started to shiver real hard—then she realized it was you. 'It's Julia,' she said, 'she's in cahoots with the devil!'"

"Shelly, that's just dumb. And it definitely is not true. Now come on." Julia stood up, presumably to put an end to the conversation and get on with the task at hand, but Shelly didn't budge. She just sat there looking up at her accusingly.

"I'm not going anywhere with you and you can't take me, either."

"Shelly, Mom's cracked okay? Don't you know that?"

"She is not, and if you try to take me from her, I'll get a butcher knife and I'll stab you."

Julia turned and looked at me. My mind raced with solutions, then went blank. The child had obviously been brainwashed and I wasn't sure what we should do. My family catastrophes had been of the more traditional variety, like: *How dare you borrow my pink sweater without asking!* Life had not prepared me for such dramas and I was sad to discover that, although my intentions were good, I was utterly useless to my friend. All I could do was tsk, shake my head, shrug my shoulders and look sympathetic.

Julia knelt down in front of Shelly and held her face in both hands. "You know my phone number, right?" No answer. Shelly's eyes shifted toward the kitchen door where Nora was leaning. I could barely make out the form of Ramon standing behind her in the half-light. He looked like he was in about the same sad shape as Nora, and I wanted out of there. They gave me the creeps.

"Right?" Julia prodded.

Shelly nodded.

"What's my number?"

Shelly rattled off our phone number as if she had just dialed it.

"You call me if you need me. If you need anything . . . understand?"

"Uh huh," she replied, lowering her eyes to look at Julia.

Julia squeezed her chin affectionately. "I love you, Shell."

"Love you too," she whispered, as she dropped her head.

"I know," Julia said, stroking her hair.

When Julia walked back toward the kitchen I was right on her heels. I was relieved Ramon was nowhere in sight. We squeezed by Nora and left through the kitchen as we had come.

Nora followed us as far as the back deck. She leaned over the railing and called out in a snide, mocking voice, "Don't forget to write!"

Julia didn't say a word until we were in the car. Then, under her breath, as we backed out of the driveway, I heard her say, "Don't worry, Mom. I won't forget a thing."

* * *

**I was greeted** at the door by a tall, skinny, stringy-haired woman with a hardness to her that was difficult not to notice. A friend of Shelly's I presumed who looked as though she had suffered some tough times of her own. On her right hip a crying two-year-old perched, slapping at her to get her attention. The young woman grabbed the little hand, shushed the child, and turned back to me.

"Hi, you Paula?" she asked, through the screen door.

I began to offer the customary greetings common in this part of the free world, when I was interrupted.

"Shelly had to run out to Quikmart. She'll be back in a few minutes." She turned her attention to the child, her back to me, and walked off leaving me standing there.

"Comeonin," she yelled back over her shoulder, as she dodged a toy car launched by Daimon, Shelly's youngest, from a makeshift runway on the coffee table. "Daimon, you start picking up these toys, NOW. I'm not telling you again," she said as she disappeared into the kitchen.

"Hi, Daimon," I said, bending at the waist to get closer to the three-year-old who, having no intention of altering his schedule of take-offs, propelled a three-inch Camaro to the left of where I was standing.

"Hi, watch this," he said excited to have an audience. He prepared another launch while Samantha, his five-year-old sister (Shelly's clone) sat two feet in front of the television wearing a plastic tiara and a white stole, mesmerized by the video, *Anastasia.* Another little girl, a little younger than Samantha, not nearly as pretty and madder than all get out, burst through the door that led from the garage into the house.

"Mommy," she screamed accusingly, "did you forget about me?" She too failed to register my presence, pushing past me on her way to the kitchen, obviously a child on a mission.

The woman with the baby still in her arms replied, "No, I haven't forgotten about you but you are still on time-out. Now get back to your room."

The little girl stomped off toward the garage beating her fists into her hips as she went. The woman with the baby turned in my direction, half-startled, as if she had just remembered something—her name, perhaps. She said, "I'm Laura. Have a seat. I'll get you some coffee."

The last thing I needed was more coffee, but Shelly's coffee was sure to be caffeinated, and I figured I needed to rev up a bit if I was going to spend any time in this chaos. I smiled weakly and looked for a spot to sit. Laura pointed to a couch piled high with clean laundry waiting to be folded and put away.

It was not a comforting home; on the contrary, after a mere three minutes I was beginning to fragment due to the overload of stimuli. My eye was unable to rest on anything soothing. The small living room was overburdened with furniture, toys and clothes, not to mention stacks of junk mail and old newspapers scattered carelessly about. Nothing matched. The couch, upholstered in frayed, cocoa-brown corduroy, wore a large crocheted orange and green afghan across its shoulders. Flanking it were two love seats, one floral in pinks and purples, the other striped in bold bands of blue and green. The floral was burdened with more laundry, the other held a smashed pizza box and a few videos. I cleared a place for myself and sat where told, on the brown couch. My coffee arrived black and in a chipped mug advertising Roadrunner Motors. Laura transferred the pizza box to the floor, stacked the videos neatly on top, and began picking through the laundry for things to fold.

I looked toward the window, mentally willing Shelly back from the Quickmart. Framing the window an abundance of houseplants competed for a glimpse of the outdoors. Unsuccessful with plants myself, I was impressed that there were no scrawny hangers-on, nothing dead or wilting, no yellowed leaves on the floor beneath them. Had the same plants been unfortunate enough to spend their days at my house, their fate would have been much different, but Shelly has always had a way with plants.

Next to one particularly robust philodendron, family photos hung cockeyed in frames that didn't necessarily fit nor compliment them. The majority were photos of the kids, all ages. Hanging in a collage frame of Shelly and Daryl's wedding, Julia looked out at me from the background of several shots. She looked less than thrilled. The marriage had been a disaster from the beginning, with Daryl being unemployed and abusive through most of it.

I watched Laura fold some very skimpy, very Frederick's-of-Hollywood lingerie. She stroked the intimate articles wistfully, almost tenderly—not unlike the way an expectant mother might handle the tiny garments intended for her unborn child. I studied her more closely. Her tall, leggy thinness, in the right light and in that lingerie, might transform her otherwise plain countenance into something alluring, at least to a hungry male willing to overlook her poor complexion and bad teeth.

She glanced over at me. "Coffee okay?" she asked.

"Mmm, yes, nice and hot," I said realizing I should try to make some sort of conversation while I impatiently awaited Shelly's return.

"So, those your kids?" I asked, sounding inane. She nodded and began the tedious story of how she had come to be living in Shelly's garage with her two kids. Her mother had kicked her out and blah blah blah . . . I tuned her out. I was not in the mood to spend my Saturday listening to another tale of woe, another '*it's not my fault my life is shit*' story. Just when Laura got to the part in her monologue where Daryl in his kindness offered her shelter, the door opened and Shelly was, thankfully and at last, home.

For all I accomplished that day, I could have skipped Sunday all together. My Saturday visit with Shelly left me flat and unmotivated. I stayed in bed until ten, resisted getting dressed at all, but eventually threw on some sweats to watch not one, but two daytime movies while I absent-mindedly sorted through trade journals and ate a whole pint of Cherry Cheesecake ice cream. It was sheer decadence on my part and dietary sabotage, not to mention the cost of delivery—an unnecessary extravagance. I promised to run an extra three miles on the treadmill and only eat salad for the rest of the week while consoling myself by comparing my life to Shelly's.

After Shelly arrived, Laura offered to take the kids to a nearby park, so that we could have some alone time, a gesture I found surprisingly considerate for someone so lacking in social graces. Shelly couldn't say enough good about Laura. Although it was challenging for the seven of them to be co-habiting a small two-bedroom, one-bath house, Laura made herself useful by giving Shelly a reprieve from the kids. A little probing was all it took to figure out that Daryl was, once again, unemployed. He picked up odd jobs here and there, Shelly said, when an opportunity arose, but basically he watched the kids while Shelly put in forty-plus hours on an assembly line at Hewlett Packard. As usual, they were having a hard time making ends meet. "Does she pay you rent," I asked.

"No, but that's okay. Like I said, she looks after the kids."

"What about Mr. Mom? I thought that was his job."

"Well, they do overlap sometimes, but it's good to have her here in case he gets called for work. Anyway, he's in a better mood when she's around, isn't on my case nearly as much."

I had a hard time visualizing Daryl in any mood besides snarly, but before I could ask for the details Shelly got to the point of our visit. "I've decided to leave him for good."

"Best news I've heard in a while. Are you serious this time?"

"Paula," she said in a pleading tone, "I've been blinded by his manipulative ways one time too many. I'm serious as a heart attack. I can't wait to see the last of his sorry ass."

"Okay, so what's the plan?"

"Well, that's why I wanted to see you. I don't make enough money to swing it on my own. Daryl will never pay child support and day care alone for two kids would cost me nearly half of what I take home each month."

"But if you get divorced, he'll be ordered to pay child support."

"Ordered and actually getting the money out of Daryl are two distinctly separate things," she said and I couldn't dispute her logic.

"I need assisted housing through the County. Otherwise I just won't be able to afford a place to live. I already applied and used the neighbor's address, so Daryl won't find out until it's over and done."

"I do know someone in that department, and with the threat of violence in the home you could conceivably get pushed up the list. I have to warn you though, there are long, and I mean long, waiting lists."

"I know, that's why I thought that if you could do anything, anything at all, Paula, I'd be eternally grateful. I just don't know how much longer I can take living with him. He absolutely drives me crazy. I get so mad sometimes I could just kill him."

I couldn't promise anything, but I told her I'd make a few phone calls and let her know. She obviously didn't know about Julia's wedding, and once again, I didn't have the heart to tell her. I told myself if Julia had wanted her sister to know, she would have sent her an invitation.

Felicia Welton was an extremist. Everything about her shouted. Her artificial cleavage was framed by a hot pink St. John suit and jeweled by Cartier.

She craved attention, but couldn't make up her mind what sort of attention she wanted. From the stories she told me I suspected that the admiration of her church community for her good works, although satisfying, didn't quite compare to the satisfaction she received from seducing an attractive young man.

Chanel No. 5 preceded her entry and would cling to my office furniture long after her departure. She shifted from one bony hip to the other, uncrossing and re-crossing her short legs. She attempted a gesture of running her hand through her hair, a feat not easily accomplished when one's hair is teased and lacquered to render it immobile in a thirty-knot wind.

She cleared her throat to draw my attention. "I went to a Sex Addict's Anonymous meeting last Tuesday," she said boldly, happy to be providing her therapist with something new to chew on. I snapped to. I didn't generally daydream in session, and frankly I'm a good listener with an exceptional memory for details but lately I found my thoughts wandering. *Probably time for a vacation. My clients deserve better than this.* As usual these days my thoughts had been of Julia. Since the invitation, I'd expected her to arrive unannounced at my office at any moment. After all, it is a little tough to plan a wedding from Bali, or wherever the hell she is these days, and December was just around the corner. Julia always made her own rules, usually on the spot to fit whatever was taking place at the moment, but this felt odd. I had to admit, I was beginning to worry, and it was affecting my practice.

"You did what?"

"Uh huh. Over at Memorial every Tuesday—S.A.A."

"And you went?" I tried to visualize the esteemed Mrs. Charles Welton at an S.A.A. meeting.

"Yes, I did," she declared in her straightforward take-charge voice, swinging a Gucci pump from her perfectly pedicured toe.

"Tell me about it." Now she had me. I was fully engaged.

"I walked into this drab little room somewhere in the basement of the hospital, way away from everything else. They're probably worried that unless they keep us sex addicts isolated, they'll find us fornicating with whatever patients we happen to bump into on our way to the meeting." She laughed. I didn't.

"Us sex addicts, Felicia? That's a pretty big diagnosis."

"Well, let me finish," she went on, bursting to talk about her little walk on the wild side. "So, I walk into this shabby little smoke-filled room with ten downtrodden, seedy individuals all gathered around this table, not looking anywhere but down at their laps. You know, Paula, there just wasn't any eye contact in that room, whatsoever."

I had to smile at the image of Felicia trying to make friends at a S.A.A. meeting, extending her pampered hand to the others in an attempt at comradery. Maybe she hoped to meet some other matronly community pillar who couldn't keep her hands off the boys. She was good hearted, but the woman just couldn't decide if she wanted to head the church auxiliary or be the heroine in a romance novel. *How sad to reach the golden years and still not know yourself.*

"Then, the leader had everyone introduce themselves. Remember that show *What's My Line*?"

"Yes."

"Where the contestants each have a turn saying, 'No, I'm Joe Blow. I'm the real Chimney Sweep!'"

"Yes, I remember."

"That's how we introduced ourselves, one after the other. 'I'm Sue Kelly and I'm a Sex Addict—I'm Winona Rider and I'm a Sex Addict.'"

"Winona Rider was there?"

"Winona somebody or another. 'I'm Humbert Whiffledick and I'm a Sex Addict.'"

I could see she was enjoying herself, but I made a point of looking at my watch to signal her to get on with it.

"They all seemed so definite and sure," she said glancing out the window wistfully.

"And when it came your turn?"

"I simply stated, 'I'm Barbara Boxer and I'm not sure if I'm a Sex Addict or not.'"

"You said you were Barbara Boxer?"

"Well, I couldn't use my real name, could I? Anyway, I tried to explain my situation further, but the leader cut me off, just like that." She snapped her fingers in the air above her head for emphasis. "After we all had an opportunity to proclaim our addiction, the leader brought out this big white timer. We each had five minutes to vent. Of course, everyone talked faster and faster when the timer began to close in on their story." Her eyes widened and she leaned in conspiratorially. I couldn't help but lean in too. "I had to suffer through the rambling of seven degenerates before my turn," she said with her hands splayed to make the point. "Stuff like, 'I only masturbated twenty times this week.' 'Oh, good for you, Malcolm!' or, my favorite: 'I had a bit of a relapse this week and had sex with a black Chippendale dancer, on the ground, in back of the KitKat club.' I was tempted to make up something, just to keep the momentum."

"What would be the point," I asked. "To entertain? To fit in?"

Felicia squirmed, drummed her fingernails and gazed out the window. "I've decided I'm not a sex addict after all."

I had to restrain myself from saying, "Of course your not a sex addict! You're a spoiled hedonist with no self control!"

Instead, I said, "How did you reach that conclusion?"

"Easy. I'm not one of them." She made exaggerated quotation marks around the words *one of them* to emphasize her superior social status. "Those people were too weird and scary. Truth be known, I was afraid to walk back to my car for fear one would masturbate on my leg or something," she said, stroking her calf and looking pitiful.

"What did you do?"

"Instead of filing out to the parking lot alongside the rest of them, I took a left turn and ended up getting lost in the bowels of the hospital."

"Oh oh," I said sympathetically.

She examined a nail on her left hand. "It turned out all right, actually. I ran into this cute janitor who . . ."

I glanced again at my watch as Felicia wrapped up her latest adventure. In the next room, my secretary put the cap back on her nail polish and answered the call for which I had been waiting.

* * *

**Across town**, Shelly walked in on Daryl and Laura. Laura was wearing a cheesy Frederick's french maid's uniform. When Shelly found her voice, she said simply and calmly, "Laura, if you intend to play french maid in this house, I suggest you start with the kitchen." She turned her back on the two of them, grabbed her coat and purse, and yelled back over her shoulder, "And don't forget to polish the silver!"

She was calling from San Diego where she planned to stay for a few days with friends before driving up the coast. We made a phone date for later that evening after I finished seeing patients and could get home, change into my sweats, grab a bottle of Chardonnay and settle into some serious catching up. She started off with a thumbnail sketch of how she had spent the last two years—the first few months wandering the back streets of Paris, losing herself in the museums and galleries, developing a taste for dark, rich coffee and buttery croissants.

"Is that where you met the man you intend to marry?"

"What man?" she said laughing.

I let it slide, enjoying the unraveling, knowing she'd get to it in her own time. Tired of Paris, she spent time traveling through Europe, looking for a place to light. We talked for three hours that first night, and by the end of our conversation I knew where she had been, what she had been through, but I knew nothing about the man in her life or why she felt both reluctant and compelled to marry . . . again. Naturally I had expected something along the lines of *"and that's when I saw him sitting there at this quaint little sidewalk café in Montmarte . . .*"

Instead, when we both sighed simultaneously, a signal which indicated the high points had been covered, she told me the real reason she was calling.

She had returned to Manzanillo, where she'd first met Turner seven years ago. She was hoping to somehow find something of him there, something of that romantic storm that had swept them up and sealed their fate. Instead she found only remnants of her past, and no matter how she assembled them, she was unable to turn the pieces into a cohesive picture. The motorcycle accident that had taken Turner's life was naturally unexpected and devastating for Julia. But I hadn't realized until just then that losing her husband had caused her to slow down long enough to review and analyze the mental movie of her life, and what she saw projected there was deeply disturbing. So I was flattered, and not at all surprised when she told me she wanted to utilize my professional services.

"Paula, I know this is a lot to ask, but as you know, I'm having a wedding in a few months and I really feel like I need to get some old stuff cleared up before I take this next step. You can say no if you want to—for any reason," she assured me, "I'll understand if you can't; there's a lot of ground to cover and I'm afraid it might take up a bit of your time over the next month. And, just so we're clear, I insist on paying you full fare."

"Julia, I couldn't charge you. And as for having the time, well, I think I might have that one figured out." I had planned on taking some time off at the end of the month anyway—already had the coverage.

"If you won't take my money, then I won't do it. Period." I could tell by her tone that she was serious; there would be no negotiation on this point.

"We'll work something out," I assured her. I told her to stay put. Stay in southern California. I knew that we needed some time away from all things familiar, including Shelly and her problems, if we were to make some significant headway in the short time we had allowed ourselves. The next day I booked us a suite at the Malibu Beach Inn, but as luck would have it we would have to wait until the end of the week for a vacancy. It worked out all right, as I had some lose ends to tie up before I could leave guilt free. By Thursday I had arranged for Deborah, my neighbor's daughter, to house sit, my paperwork was under control, and I was trying to contain my excitement over seeing Julia again. Friday afternoon, after the coast was clear at the office, I could hop in my Volvo and head south. I figured that if I could break away before lunch, I could make it to Malibu in time to join her for dinner that evening.

* * *

**My pager went off** Thursday evening, just as I was finishing up at the gym. It was Charles Welton's secretary calling to inform me that Felicia had just been admitted to St. Mary's Hospital and requesting that I please stop in to see her as soon as possible. I assured the woman that I would go right away, when I remembered that St. Mary's is in San Francisco.

"What's happened?" I asked. "Why is she in a San Francisco hospital?"

"That's where it occurred."

"What? What occurred?"

"San Francisco is where she was raped."

I changed back into my work clothes and picked up a strawberry protein smoothy from the juice bar on my way out of the gym. It would keep me company and stave off hunger while I drove down to the city to check on Felicia. The timing on this was not good. Of course one could argue that there is never a great time to experience a rape, but from a practical standpoint, if she was going to get herself raped, I would have preferred it happen when I was going to be in town.

* * *

**By the time I got to the hospital** I'd had plenty of time to chastise myself for not being more stern with her: *Felicia, you mustn't . . . Haven't you heard of sexually transmitted . . . You What? . . . Are you out of your mind?* I ran through all the things I could have, should have said to caution her, to make her take her actions more seriously. I never thought she would put herself in harm's way, imagining her wealth and social status a buffer against the barbarous and repugnant.

Over the years I've managed to streamline my practice. Jumping on the healthy body/healthy mind bandwagon early on I've been able to attract a client base who are in fine whack; meaning those who suffer from major psychosis usually find their way to other professionals. No one in my practice is suicidal, as far as I know, and the majority of my cases consist of couples in need of counseling, the neurotic socialite in search of a safe place to recount her daily trials and tribulations, and menopausal women who can't figure out why they've suddenly gone crazy. Throw in the occasional fifteen-year-old girl in the midst of a prom/boyfriend/identity crisis and you have a pretty accurate profile of those in my care. My clients don't generally end up in hospitals unless they're in an auto accident or need a tummy tuck.

I didn't know what condition Felicia would be in, whether or not she was going to need further hospitalization, if I needed to arrange a transfer to a Sonoma County hospital, or if she'd be in such bad shape that I'd be expected to postpone my meeting with Julia until she stabilized. Compounding my guilt for not being a more astute practitioner was the sure knowledge that regardless of Felicia's state, I *was* leaving tomorrow, leaving a client who had just been assaulted, to meet my long-lost best friend. I know what Charlotte, my replacement, would say: "When are they not in crisis?" Still, it had me rattled. Rattled and guilty. Two of my least favorite emotions.

I parked on the second level of the underground garage and hopped on the first elevator that presented itself. The elevator was already occupied by a teenage boy and girl with spiked hair who shared matching nose rings, a private joke and a helium-filled balloon that congratulated a new mother. The only other occupant was an elderly well-groomed gentleman holding a bouquet of red roses close to his chest. His aftershave, Bay Rum, filled the car and reminded me of my grandfather and our Sunday afternoon strolls into town to share a banana split. In order to breathe him in, I stood as close to him as elevator etiquette would allow. He cleared his throat often and held the door for me as I left. I tried to catch his eye when I thanked him, but his thoughts were elsewhere. He gave me what he could—a slight nod before burying his face in the roses.

The elevator door closed on a sweet memory and I returned to the task at hand. I moved purposefully toward the nurses station but before reaching it I realized my mistake. I had become so wrapped up in the memory of my grandfather that I had inadvertently gotten off on the wrong floor: Oncology. Not where I needed to be. I stopped, spun around to head back toward the elevator, when I practically toppled a little bald-headed old lady behind me who was trying, rather unsuccessfully, to make her way down the hall in one of those walkers that look like they're more trouble than they're worth.

"I'm so sorry!" I said, bending to help steady her on her feet. "I should have been looking where I was going."

She glared up at me and shaking off my proffered assistance, blared caustically and loud enough to turn heads at the nurse's station: "I was doing pretty well until you slammed into me!"

I straightened up and apologized for a second time as bull dog woman yelped for her nurse while making a big to-do of trying to re-plant herself in the walker.

There was something about her voice that stirred a memory. I looked into her eyes and my mouth dropped open. *Couldn't be. But, it sure looks like her.* "Nora?" I asked, holding her walker steady, while she scanned my face, looking for clues as to who I might be.

Her eyes narrowed and her nose scrunched up as if she had just smelled something unsavory. "How do you know my name?" she demanded.

Visions of her pounding Julia's head into the kitchen wall flooded my mind's eye, giving me an instant headache. I covered my eyes with the palms of my hands trying to block out the images, but they kept coming: pale legs dripping blood, backside bruised and swollen, preteen Julia huddling on the floor of her mother's closet.

"What's going on here?" Nora's nurse inquired.

I snapped to and realized I had to get away from Nora as quickly as possible. "Sorry, excuse me," I said to the nurse. And to Nora, "I beg your pardon, you just look like someone I use to know," I said lamely and rushed off toward the elevator.

"But you know my name! Who are you?!" she yelled after me, throwing herself into a coughing fit.

She was gasping for breath by the time the elevator door finally closed.

# *Julia:*

Memories of my mother have taken on a particular color in my mind's eye. They are a sort of a pale taupe now. But when I was three, four and even five years old, my mother was the sun. Before we had our own cottage, I lived with my grandparents, Nana and Baba, and only saw my mother on the weekends. She'd swing through the front door Saturday morning in some pink or yellow-flowered sun dress, curls piled up on top of her head, smelling like Juicy Fruit, Pall Malls and Coty's Tigress perfume. She'd scoop me up, plop me down on the seat next to her in her '40 Ford convertible and off we'd go, singing our heads off. "Side by Side" was our favorite song. And it was true we didn't have a barrel of money, like the song says, but we had each other and that was enough for me.

Sometimes we'd go to the beach. After a great deal of splashing around at the water's edge, dodging imaginary sea monsters and sandcastle building, we'd eat our tuna fish sandwiches and later, while she'd lay out sunning herself, I'd fall asleep on a white sheet, feeling the warmth of the sand beneath me, listening to the waves and sucking on a strand of my saltwatered hair. More times than not I was awakened when some toothy, tanned fellow plopped down next to my mother and proceeded to woo her with his wit or impress her by walking on his hands or performing some other feat of amazement. He always thought I was her sister, which delighted her no end. She wasn't good at sending him away, and if he hung around too long, we'd have to get up and leave the beach just to shake him.

Our day cut short would tend to put me in a snit, so she'd make it up to me with a stopover at Bob's Big Boy. She worked there part time as a carhop during the week, so I could fill up on chocolate malts and fries to my heart's content without it costing her a red cent. She never ate a single french fry—had to watch her figure, you know. But I'd eat till I was full as a tick and she'd just smile at me, content to wait until I was done. Anyhow, the waiting gave her an opportunity to gossip away the rest of the day with the other carhops.

Sunday nights I was disconsolate when it was time for her to leave. I knew that when she wasn't working as a carhop she had *gigs*. I didn't know what gigs were, only that they made her happy. Aside from that, I couldn't imagine where she went or what her life was like without me. And without her, my life felt slow-moving and drab. I didn't like us being apart and dreamt up numerous scenarios designed to keep her with me. I feigned illness, and once made a miniature bed in a matchstick box—a bed for her little toe. I reasoned that if her toe stayed, so would she.

She never visited much with my grandparents when she came. Usually she'd breeze in, scoop me up and off we'd go for a drive. When we weren't out driving around and singing, we played dolls on the floor of my room with Betsy Wetsy and Lambchop as unlikely cohorts involved in adventures she'd dream up on the spot to make me giggle. When she'd had enough of that she'd read to me from her movie magazines. It was in those pages that I got my first glimpse of the glamourous life for which my mother yearned. We rummaged the pages for just the right hairstyles. She'd pull out her assortment of hair combs and we'd get to work. Once Mom felt she had achieved the starlet look, she'd start on me. I never cared much how I looked, so I wasn't very particular how the hairdo turned out. I just loved the feel of her hands in my hair.

At other times, if the sun was out, we'd put on our bathing suits and lie next to each other on matching lounge chairs in the backyard. I had little heart-shaped sunglasses she insisted I wear. Hers were black and so large they would have made great white circles around her eyes if she wasn't careful to keep shifting them around. We'd lie for hours sunning ourselves, slathered up in baby oil and iodine, listening to her favorite jazz station on the radio. At some point she'd sit up, study her watch and announce us baked. I was the tannest four-year-old in all of Los Angeles. My grandmother would bite her lip and shake her head when I slid into the kitchen to show off my line where the brown skin met the white.

* * *

**My mother had a friend**, Steve Tyler, who was a struggling, but sometimes successful TV producer. He invited her on set more than once, fueling her theatrical aspirations. They had gone to Montebello High School together and he had always had a crush on her. Her only interest in Steve was that their association might benefit her. She lived in hopes of someday being discovered. She knew some very big stars had been discovered in unlikely locales such as corner drug stores or a particular coffee shop in Santa Monica. She told me it was just a matter of time until it was her turn. "I have the look," she'd explain to me, and I had to agree that she did seem to resemble the women in the magazines, at least as far as their hair was concerned. Because her good fortune was lurking around the corner she never left the house without looking like she was ready to step onto a movie set. I always believed her; she said it would happen so I knew it would, but I really started getting excited over the eventuality of her stardom after she took me to see her favorite movie, *Gone With The Wind.* It was then I finally understood why she was so passionate about her future movie career. As far as I could tell, my mother was a dead ringer for Scarlett O'Hara. We practiced "speaking Southern" for weeks after, until Nana, tired of me calling her Mammie, put an end to my affected Southern belle ways.

In 1954 Steve Tyler produced a hit show which aired on Wednesday evenings called the *I Want To Get Married Show.* Momma told me that she was going to be in the audience one night, so I threw a tantrum until Nana agreed to let me stay up to watch the show in the hopes of catching a glimpse of her, something Nana assured me was highly unlikely. The theme of the show centered on four contestants who tried to convince a panel of celebrities that they were the most deserving of a spouse. The winner won a date with a mystery guest, usually a model or some minor film star. They won prizes too, like beauty products, toasters or other small appliances for the women, and shaving products and tool kits for the men. The big thing of course was the date.

The show began with a close up of one contestant after another stating to the world "I want to get married." That night, the fourth contestant called at the last minute to say her boyfriend had proposed to her to keep her from going on the show and she wouldn't be able to make it. With only twenty minutes to air time, Steve grabbed my mother and insisted she fill in. She protested briefly, but only because of a sudden unexpected case of stage fright. In front of the camera, she looked scared to death as she announced timidly to the viewing audience, including our shocked family, "I want to get married."

Later in the show she had the opportunity to state her case, which I was happy to hear included her darling four-year-old daughter, so bright and talented. Whether because of the panel's sympathy for a young woman raising a daughter on her own, or just my mother's star quality, Mom won a date that evening with the current Mr. Universe. When he walked on stage every woman in the audience gasped, including Nana and including my mother. I gasped too, as it seemed the thing to do. Nothing really came of the date. It turned out he was a homosexual, or that's what my mother told the girls at Bob's Big Boy, she could tell by his lack of interest in her on their one and only date.

She was never discovered, at least not in the way she had hoped. She should have forgotten about the movie business and concentrated on her God-given talent as a jazz musician. Although I was unaware of it at the time, she was one hell of a keyboard player and when she wasn't playing dolls with me she played with some soon-to-be All Time Greats, like Dave Brubeck and Chetty Baker. It was due to her late-night, cigarette-smoking, scotch-drinking ways that I lived with my grandparents. And it was this lifestyle of hers that caused friction between her and Nana. With her talent and looks, doors would have swung open for her, if she had been smart enough to know which doors to stand in front of.

Sometimes we'd eat a big meal together in the middle of the day. Nana loved hauling out her good china and making a big production out of a meal. I don't know what prompted such occasions, but even then I knew my mother wasn't particularly excited to spend an afternoon cooking with Nana. I'd help by standing on a chair to stir pots.

"Nora," my grandmother hissed, "I need those onions chopped now, not whenever you're through talking to God-only-knows-who!"

"She's talking to God?" I whispered, reverently.

"No, sweetheart. Keep stirring."

My mother, smoking and laughing on the phone, gave Nana a slant-eyed glare and flung her arm to indicate that Nana should either silence herself or disappear—the latter being preferable. I sensed the tension building in the kitchen and stirred extra vigorously until spaghetti sauce slopped out of the pot and onto my apron.

"That's good, Julia. Here, you get down now," Nana said, lowering me to the floor. "Do you think you could lay out the cloth napkins and silver the way I taught you last time?"

"Aye Aye, Nana," I said with my best Shirley Temple little-soldier salute.

"Please don't do that, dear. You are neither in the military nor the movies."

"Okay," I said, as my mom slammed down the receiver. Looking over my shoulder I saw the two of them red faced and glaring.

* * *

**"She's not really your Grandma, honey."** We were on my twin bed playing my favorite game. I cuddled up in the crook of her arm while she drew disappearing doggies and alphabet letters in the dark with the coal of her cigarette. My job, on such evenings, was to guess her drawings. When I had trouble guessing one correctly she'd draw it on my belly with her finger. Some evenings I'd swallow my pride and miss on purpose just to feel her long red nail on my skin. The metallic sunburst medallion she wore on a chain around her neck captivated me. I'd lay stretched out beside her fingering the rays and wondering about the woman in the center. She never took it off and that was part of its fascination for me.

My tummy bulged from the chocolate cake I'd forced down after second helpings of everything except the lima beans. I managed to pop up to a kneeling position anyway.

"She's not?" I asked half-hysterically—remembering all too clearly the late-night movie we had watched where aliens paraded around in the body of loved ones, fooling everybody—expecting the alien inhabiting Nana's body to burst through the door laughing diabolically at how she'd been able to trick us into believing she was the real Nana. "WHO IS SHE?" I demanded.

"Shh, shhh," she said, pulling me back down. "Your real grandmother is beautiful, graceful and very talented. A musician, like me. Well, a conductor actually."

"Really?" My only knowledge of a conductor came from Captain Kangaroo and Mr. Greenjeans, so I naturally assumed my grandmother worked for the railroad, conducting people—while singing to them, perhaps.

"Uh huh."

"Who does she look like?"

"Loretta Young."

"Who's that?"

"The pretty woman who sweeps through the double doors in the Loretta Young Show, duh duh, dumpdedum," she sung the first few bars of the theme song and I recognized it right away.

"Oh, her. Really?"

"Yes."

"So who is Nana?" I whispered.

"She's my stepmother. Baba married her when I was ten."

"Oh. And, what's my real grandmother's name."

"Lenore."

"Like my middle name?"

"Yes, honey."

I thought awhile as my mother hummed more of the theme song, "Well, when can I meet her?"

"You can't. She's dead."

"And Nana KILLED her!" I popped up again, staring at the door, this time expecting to see this pseudo-grandmother creature coming through the door with an ax.

"No, of course not, silly."

"Really," I asked, reluctant to lie down for fear of some new revelation.

"Julia, stop saying 'really', like I'm making stuff up. You must believe everything I tell you. I'm your mother, and mothers never lie. Now, tell me, who loves you best?

"You, Mom."

"That's right. Now go to sleep."

I fell asleep that night with Loretta Young heading off into the distance on a train singing and waving farewell from the caboose, to a crowd of crying grandchildren.

When I was five, Baba died of a heart attack while putting the finishing touches on my walk-in doll house. Nana had sewn curtains to hang in the little windows, and my mother had contributed a miniature Susie Homemaker kitchen with painted-on burners and a refrigerator complete with tiny fake bottles of Coca Cola. I already had my china tea set from the previous Christmas and was anxious to move in. My new home was actually a single room about six-feet square, five-feet high, so I didn't even have to duck down to walk in. I had expected to live in this house (now that I was a big girl and soon going to kindergarten and all that) next to Nana and Baba, with my mother visiting often. Baba finished laying the wall-to-wall carpet and was busy mixing paint for the exterior.

"Baba, could it have yellow windows," I asked, supervising the work from my swing set.

"I thought you wanted a green doll house. See, that's why I have green paint here, Julia. It's too late to change your mind now."

"I still want it green. I only want the windows yellow. You know, around the edges." I was eager to move in and begin throwing tea parties and having babies like the other women in the neighborhood.

My grandfather was the only father I knew. Every weekday at four-thirty in the afternoon my grandmother brushed out my hair, cleaned me up, put me in the ruffliest dress I owned, and sat me by the window to await his return from work. It was the highlight of my day. Not only did I adore Baba but, even when he was exhausted from his job at the factory, he always stopped to buy me a little treat. He hid the surprise in his black metal lunch pail. When his truck pulled up at the front curb and he started up the walk, I burst from the door, flung myself against his overalls and reached for the pail. Inside I discovered my treasure and brought it to Nana to admire, unless of course it was candy.

"Can't we just keep it all green, honey," he asked, dipping his brush. "I really would like to finish this project today and if we don't go changing things now I have a good crack at it. I . . ." He made a face I'd never seen before, clutched his chest and crumpled over.

I was there in a flash, "Baba," I yelled, grabbing his shirt front, "we don't have to have yellow!"

Before I went to sleep that night Mom explained that Baba had gone to live at his other home and I wasn't going to see him again. Everyone cried about his leaving, but no one did anything about it. I refused to give up my ritual and every evening I sat by the window until Nana made me come to the dinner table. When my diligent waiting didn't bring him home, I spent hour after hour drawing him pictures I knew he would like. When he finally returned I wanted to be able to show him I hadn't forgotten him.

One month later my mom and I moved to a place of our own. Nana said the doll house would always be there whenever I came to visit, but we didn't come often. And I never did get to live in the little house Baba had worked on so hard.

* * *

**My mother called our new house a cottage**. In fact it was an add-on mother-in-law unit behind a larger house in the San Fernando valley. Madlyn lived in the big house with her two teenage daughters and three young sons. The boys played loud games in the driveway in front of our house. I was shy and much preferred hanging out on the living room floor with my coloring book and crayons while Mom yukked it up with her friends. She called them *the girls*. When the girls arrived, the cottage swished with taffeta until they congregated at the kitchen table where soon their cigarette smoke mingled flawlessly with their Aqua Net and toilet water. Mom was always the prettiest, and as far as I could tell, the center of attention with tales of her suitors. I hummed and colored away but I didn't fool anyone. Soon I became the little pitcher with big ears who was unceremoniously tossed to the wolves in the driveway. Mom had to literally push me out the door.

Once outside, I stopped begging and crying and began to plaster myself against the rough white stucco exterior of our house as I tried to become the invisible girl. The boys looked me over briefly and one slammed a ball off the wall next to me. My grandparents had been very protective and kept me in the house a lot. I was as accustomed to the everyday conversations of adults as I was unfamiliar with the ways of children. And now that I supposedly had my mother all to myself it seemed like a cruel twist in the plot of my life that she wasn't all that interested in having me all to herself.

"Let me in!" I yelled, banging on the front door. I didn't know then what to expect from my mother, nor how our relationship would finally turn out in the end. All I knew was that I loved her, beautiful her, with everything I knew as love. I also knew that I didn't want to know those boys. I was unprepared for the door to suddenly fly open and equally unprepared for the look on her face as she stood there, solid, behind the screen door, blocking the passage inside, her face scored by the mesh of the screen, the jagged tear in the upper right hand corner—a flag, a warning—catching my attention.

"Stop it!" she commanded, her voice steely and cold.

"I want in," I whimpered. My grandma would have scooped me up and carried me to safety and I couldn't understand why she wouldn't yield to my pleas.

"Julia, it's time you learned you don't always get everything you want." With that, the door slammed shut.

I stood staring at the closed door, the chipped white paint. I heard their laughter from within: my mother's voice whining, mimicking, more laughter. Something in me turned silently and surely, like a tumbler in a combination lock falling into position. "I don't believe you," I whispered to the doorknob.

In my dream I fly high over the heads of my schoolmates. They point and squeal, "Look at Julia! She can fly!" More children rush out onto the playground as arms spread wide, I float higher and higher above them. I hear someone shout "Damn you!" I begin to fall back to the playground, I flap my arms and strain my head toward the heavens willing myself airborne. To my dismay I tumble back into my body and wake up to the familiar sounds of home. It's the weekend and it seems that just the thought of spending two whole days in each other's company is enough to start Mom and Tom Schurr, my new stepfather, screaming at each other.

Yolanda, the teenage girl who lives next door, knows about astrology and has marked my calendar and assured me that I am special because, like her, I am a Leo and instead of a cold orb we have God's own sun to watch over us. I hugged my toy lion and looking over at the calendar, August 6, began softly singing, "Happy birthday to me." After picking out just the right dress, I made my way downstairs where I could smell breakfast had already started. I slipped into my seat quietly and placed a napkin in my lap. *They'll stop arguing once* they *notice I'm here, and shower me with birthday kisses.*

"If you could just manage to keep the goddamn dishes washed, I wouldn't have to be over here searching . . ." he broke off when he saw me sitting there silently watching them. "I wish you'd stop sneaking around like that, Julia. It seems like every time I turn around there you are."

"Sorry," I said, fiddling with my napkin.

"Sorry, who?"

"Sorry, sir."

"Look at me, when you address me."

I looked up at my new father and could tell by his face he wasn't really mad at me. Just mad at Mom. "Sorry sir," I said, straightening my back, before I was reminded about my posture too.

"Stop picking at your napkin," Mom said, as she removed dishes from the table.

"May I have some Tang, please?" She looked particularly pretty that morning, even if her face was tear streaked. At twenty-six my mother was considered a dark-haired sultry beauty. She wished she was taller, but men found her cute, witty and sexy. Her recent marriage to the 19-year-old butcher from the Piggly Wiggly was unexpected, especially to me, who had never met the man prior to his appearance in my life as my new father. Six months ago I had been left with Madlyn, and told Mommy would return on Saturday with a new dad for me. I waited at Madlyn's window all day Saturday, fussing with my hair, tying and retying the bows of my shoes. I knew how it would be: They would pull up to the curb and walk arm-in-arm up the walkway, laughing and happy. I would run out to them, as I had my grandfather. My new dad, who would look like Rhett Butler, would pick me up and swing me around. "Our little girl," they'd say in unison, and we'd drive off together singing, "Side by Side."

The actual event was not so grand. At nine o'clock they still had not arrived, and Madlyn put me to bed. I met Tom the next morning at breakfast. He wasn't a thing like Rhett. He was quiet and withdrawn as he moved his scrambled eggs around his plate. My mother was close to frantic, bringing him ketchup, grape jelly and refilling his coffee cup. I wasn't sure what was expected of me. I made sure my bangs weren't in my eyes and sucked on my lips to keep from saying the wrong thing. I guess she had been waiting for him to acknowledge me in some way so that we could get on with the business of being a happy family. She sat between the two of us, glancing back and forth to both of us as she sipped her coffee. Finally she grabbed my hand with her left and reached for Tom's hand with her right.

"Tom, I'd like you to meet my daughter, Julia," her smile so broad I could see gold fillings in her teeth I hadn't known were there. "Julia, Tom is your new stepfather," she whispered to me, holding her head at an odd angle, blocking Tom's expression from my view.

I raised up out of my seat to see him better over my mother's head. "Hello, Tom," I said, looking into his dark brown eyes.

"Hello, Julia. You can call me Dad if you like." My mother relaxed back into her chair, relieved, and began planning a day at the park for the three of us. It took me five weeks of practicing in the mirror before I got up the nerve to call him Dad. It wasn't easy. He didn't act like a dad. It was clear as the weeks went by that he was most interested in being my mother's lover, and her having a child was something for him to endure for the privilege. Having never had a father, I accepted his aloof attitude as being just the way men are and set about showing him reasons to find me irresistible.

"I think I have something in my eye," I said presenting him with the blue-violet of my eyes. "I know what eight-times-four is," I'd announce peering over the top of his newspaper. I even resorted to knock-knock jokes, hoping to wow him with my shining personality. Usually he'd just give me a look that seemed to mean, "Are you still here?" The more I tried, the more apparent it became that he had little use for me. I was not happy when he yelled at my mother, either. Nor was I happy about how I was being pushed aside for their private time.

My mother sat a glass of Tang in front of me. "Julia, that's a school dress you're wearing."

"Yes, Mam." I was having a hard time getting used to calling her Mam, but that was what we did now that we had a dad. Mam. It reminded me of Spam and I was hard pressed not to giggle at first.

"Did you forget it's Saturday?"

"But I thought . . ." I couldn't bring myself to remind her it was my birthday. "Umm, I guess I wasn't thinking. I'll take it off," I pushed back from the table.

"No, wear it. It looks nice on you. Just don't get it dirty."

I smiled at her with what I thought of as our private smile and reached for the last pancake. Remembering my manners in the nick of time, I left the pancake for my mother and got up to make one for myself. I poured a backwards 6 into the skillet, and when the batter started to bubble, poured more on top of it, making myself a birthday pancake. I turned the pancake over, and while it cooked, I daydreamed about the Suzy Homemaker bake set I wanted for my present. Mom and Tom left the table so I took advantage of their absence to drown my pancake in maple syrup and top it off with a squirt of whipped cream.

By the time I finished rinsing my plate, I could hear sounds that meant they were having their private time again. I tiptoed over to the door, trying to figure out what they did during private time. "Send her to the store." "I can't. It's five miles away. Ever since you moved us out here, there's nowhere to send her."

The door opened a crack and I pretended to be passing by to my room. Inside I could see Tom lying on the bed in his underwear. My mother's head suddenly appeared in the crack.

"Julia," she said, behind the half-closed door, "Tell you what, I was going to keep this a surprise but, well, your cousins are coming for a visit today."

"Linda, too?" I asked, excited now as the birthday plan began to reveal itself.

"Uh huh. But they've never been here before and I'm afraid they'll get lost."

"Oh no! What do we do?"

"Hmm, what do you think?" she paused, giving me time to come up with something. I shrugged as big as I could and craned my neck to peek around her and into the bedroom. She took hold of my shoulders, tugging on my line of vision until we were eye to eye. "I know!" she said, snapping her fingers as she supplied the solution. "If you wait for them down at the end of the street, they'll know where to turn. OK?"

"OK. What time are they coming?"

"Not sure. It could be a while, or . . ." she looked at her watch and gasped, "God, it could be any minute."

"I'll go right now!"

"Good idea. Take a sweater. It could get cold later on."

*That's not too likely*, but I took a sweater and my lion, and went out the back door. I was a few steps down the walk when I heard the unmistakable sound of the door locking. I was startled for a second. Then I realized the obvious: *She's going to make me a cake.*

If I had learned anything from my mother it was how to treat house guests. I rehearsed my hostess speech: *So good of you to come . . . Care for some chocolate milk? . . . Oh, Linda, You shouldn't have.* Hours passed. I perched myself on a large rock at the side of the road, dressed the lion in my sweater, made up games in the dirt, and tried to stay clean. I imagined my cousins coming in their truck, bringing lots of presents. *Maybe they'll bring Sadie, the cocker spaniel.* Then I heard a truck. I stood up and edged out into the road to get a better look. The truck slowed, stopped. A dirty looking man moved over to the passenger side of the truck, rolled down the window, and said, "Are you lost little girl?"

"No, I'm just waiting for my cousins, but they probably got lost. It's my birthday and my mom's decorating for my party, and making a cake—a chocolate one. There'll be lots of presents too." The man made me edgy and I felt like an explanation was in order.

"Your birthday, huh? That there your birthday dress?" I nodded. "Turn around let me see how pretty you look." I spun around as fast as I could. "No, turn around slow-like so I can get a good look at your party dress. How old are you today?"

"I'm six," I flushed, turning slowly. *Mind your elders.* Well, he was an adult, and I was busy practicing manners these days. Nonetheless, I didn't particularly like him admiring my dress.

"What's your name, birthday girl?" he said in a deep voice, his face getting more and more red as he spoke.

"Julia O'Hara," I lied.

"Are you going to have milk with your cake?" His eyes were glazing over in a weird way. The more red and glazed he looked, the faster I talked.

Why he needed to know about the milk I couldn't guess, but that didn't keep me from rounding out the menu for him. "Sure, milk, probably Pepsi and 7-up too. We always have an assortment of beverages when company comes." Just then his head snapped back and he said in a low, panting voice, as he pushed open the car door, "Here's some milk for your party Julia O'Hara." I looked down and sure enough his private part, red and throbbing, was squirting milk out onto the side of the street. He started laughing as I grabbed up my lion and ran down the dirt road to our duplex. I looked back once as I ran, to see if the man was following me. He was nowhere in sight. Breathless, I got to the kitchen door as fast as I could, only to find the door still locked. Not only was I afraid but I suddenly had to pee and I was hungry, starving in fact. I rattled the door, "Mommy!"

Inside, and unbeknown to me at the time, my parents slept the sleep of the sexually satiated, the sleep of the drugged. It was four in the afternoon and they would sleep another two hours before arising and feeling guilty. She wouldn't remember until the next day that it had been my birthday, being too caught up in her new life and her new husband with his kinky games.

* * *

**Joan Davis had seen enough.** "Julia, come over here child, what are you fussing about? Aren't your parents home?"

"Joan, stay out of this," her husband said from his chair in the living room, "You'll just make trouble for the girl."

"But she's been out there all day!" Joan said under her breath.

I shuffled over to the next door neighbor, kicking a rock with my patent leather shoes, not caring any more if I stayed spotless for the party that wasn't going to happen anyway.

"May I use your bathroom, Mrs. Davis? I think they're sleeping," I offered by way of explanation. It was just too embarrassing to say anything more.

"Of course, dear. And we have some fried chicken here if you'd like some," she said, sending a chastising, disapproving glare to our kitchen door, as she closed her own.

"Thank you. It smells good," I said as I emerged from the bathroom, sat my sweatered toy lion in a chair, then took a seat between the two of them at the Davis' kitchen table.

"Well yes, you sit right on down here, Julia. Pretty dress, dear," she said adjusting my chair for me. At that my manners flew out the window and my lip started quivering from the embarrassment of it all. I started picking at my napkin.

"After you finish that I have some homemade chocolate cake, if you're interested?"

I had to squeeze my lips together tight to keep the sounds in. I sat staring at my hands, unable to speak, while Mrs. Davis continued being kind, loading up my plate and murmuring softly, consoling, encouraging me to eat. "Julia honey? Julia?"

We moved a lot, which meant I was never able to get settled in with a group of friends. I was destined to always be the new kid. By the time I approached my seventh birthday I had already attended three different schools and was closing in on my fourth.

My mother had great faith in my innate sense of direction. The day before I was to make an appearance at the new school, she would drive me there, pointing out certain landmarks where I was to turn left or right. "Got it?" she'd ask. "Got it," I'd reply. And the next day I was on my own. "If you get lost, just ask a friend on the street," she'd say. It was never clear to me which of the people I'd encounter on my morning walk were the friends that she spoke of, and which were the strangers I was suppose to avoid. The upshot being that I got there on my own. Sometimes it'd take me twice as long as it should have, but I'd get there eventually, arriving with a satisfying new familiarity of the surrounding area.

Once there, I'd march straight to the office and get myself registered. That's how I ended up with the last name of Schurr. I simply told them my name was Julia Schurr, and it became a fact.

After about a month of living my life with an alias, I got called into the office of Miss Taylor, a young school counselor, who was prone to bending the rules if she thought it was in the best interest of a child.

"Julia, it seems your last school has no record of a Julia Schurr."

"Really?"

"Do you know why that might be?"

I took a minute to try to find the right words. "It's probably because I've had a name change."

"Oh? And how's that?"

"Well, my mother married Tom Schurr," I said confidently as if that bit of news would put an end to the questions. It didn't.

"Did Mr. Schurr adopt you?"

"Not yet."

"Did the courts change your name?"

"No," I said, beginning to fidget.

"So, let's see. Your new father's last name is Schurr," she said. I nodded. "And your mother's new last name is Schurr also?" I nodded again. "And you want to have the same last name as your mom and stepfather, right?"

If I'd been older, I would have told her that my mother was slipping away from me, her attention having drifted over to her new husband who was incapable of loving her in the way she desired. If I could have found the words, I would have told her that I hated it that she had discarded *our* last name to take *his*. I could have said I felt discarded too, like I was in the way. But I was a child, so instead I said: "Yes, that's it."

"OK," she said. Simple as that. I left her office a few inches taller and fully prepared to conquer any and all obstacles set before me. I remained Julia Schurr until I married thirteen years later.

Their passion for each other was more dark than light, more greedy than giving. My mother's popularity with her fellow musicians and her late-night jam sessions fanned the ember of Tom's jealousy into a blinding, raging flame. He took a baseball bat to her piano to emphasize the severity of his discontent. I remember the day well. Having never seen violence on television nor witnessed it in any form I was ill-prepared to cope. My natural instinct told me to run . . . but then, there was my mother frantically trying to pull him away from her treasure, her only source of consistent gratification. Her screams and pleas were ineffectual against his furor as he smashed and splintered that poor upright. When there was little left to do but sweep up the kindling, she collapsed on the floor in the kitchen weeping while he tore her music to shreds, screaming words I didn't understand. All the while I stood in front of my crouched mother, watching his every move and shielding her from the hateful words he hurled at her.

Somewhere in the midst of his fury, his eyes met mine. I can't say what he saw, but something in my accusing stare caused him to slowly walk over to the bookshelf and pull down one of my mother's photo albums; the one she had discreetly placed amongst her romance novels. While glaring at both of us, he proceeded to dislodge and rip apart photo after photo. I didn't understand the significance then, but years later when I asked to see a photo of my father, the only one she could produce was a pasted together snapshot taken in Tijuana where he and some other boys, all in comically huge sombreros, mugged for the camera. The handsome blonde youth in the back was my father. I had only met him once, briefly when I was five, and that hadn't gone too well as far as I was concerned. So I really didn't know much about him. After seeing the photo with him in the hat, I thought maybe he was a Mexican. My mother explained that was not the case. So from then on I just thought of him as "my father in the sombrero."

On that day—that one hot L.A. afternoon—baseball bat in hand, Tom Schurr put to rest any dream my mother had ever imagined for herself. Her dreams were thin and narrow then and easily torn. That day he seized her life and set the tone for what she would become by stamping her hopes invalid and claiming her life for himself. Her surrender wasn't complete until music had been banished from our lives. That meant dancing had to go too. And dancing was the one last thing my mother and I did together that would always end in us throwing our heads back and laughing as we whirled and dipped—two girls cutting a mean rug.

* * *

**After that I started believing** that it was my fault he landed smack dab in the middle of our lives. First grade, before I had ever heard anything about Tom Schurr or knew that a stepfather was in my future, Miss Baldwin pointed to a flattened globe made into a wall poster entitled, *Our World and Her People*, which spread across one whole wall of our classroom. She pointed out the different countries and explained what ancestors were. The ancestors were represented by small couples, hand-in-hand, clothed in native garb and randomly sprinkled across the map. Our assignment was to go home and find out from our parents where our ancestors had lived.

My mom was fixing dinner for the two of us when I burst in, play-streaked, through the kitchen door and asked the question. I was excited. It was my first homework assignment. Without looking up from the cutting board or pausing in any way, she responded, "You're French and Russian."

My heart stood still. "Are you sure?" I asked, knowing she was sometimes forgetful.

"Of course I'm sure," she laughed.

*RUSSIAN!* At my age I didn't know much, but I had made it a point to eavesdrop on adult conversations whenever possible and I knew beyond a doubt that to the majority of Los Angeleans in the 1950's, Russians were evil. I didn't know why, I just knew I would be the source of horrific ridicule and ostracization if I placed my flag on that map in the Union of Soviet Socialists. No way. I couldn't do it. A pang of guilt struck and a little voice said something that sounded like a child's version of "You'll be denouncing your father." I had a fitful sleep that night. I slept with my mother back then and to soothe me she stroked my back with her fingernails, softly, until I finally drifted off.

The next day I dragged myself to school. I didn't know what I would do until the actual moment when Miss Baldwin asked in front of everyone, "and Julia La Chance, where are your parents from?"

"France and . . ." I hesitated while she wrote my name on a little flag.

"Just France? Anywhere else?"

"Germany," I replied. I waited for her to stand up, walk over and smack me for lying. *You are not a German, Julia. How dare you parade as one*!" Instead she unflinchingly wrote my name on another flag, and handed them both to me to stab on the map. In my mind, Germany was somehow in the same general category as Russia—only more acceptable. I wasn't sure what linked them, something to do with a war, I thought. My guilt stayed with me for months later and I prayed that the hideous *Our World and Her People* would disappear before someone found me out.

Instead God decided to punish me with Tom Schurr, a German, who shortly thereafter invaded my life and changed my relationship with my mother forever.

I took to the stage for solace. Not a real stage, but real enough. When I was nine, we lived in an old wooden house with a big front porch and a detached garage. The garage was sheltered by an overgrown willow tree whose branches obscured the roof top and one whole side of the building, providing the perfect retreat where I could act out a life of my own choosing without being noticed. It was there I became *Aphrodite, Goddess of Love,* or some other sought after character who was loved by all. Safely hidden I'd perform the dual roles of both the lover and the beloved. When Elizabeth, the seven-year-old two doors down, was around I'd enlist her into my cast of characters.

* * *

**It had fallen upon me** to walk her to school every day. She was a spoiled, pampered child, with her hair tightly braided and bowed, her dresses crisp and flouncy. I didn't care for her much. Not only was she younger than I, but I hated the way she bounced when she walked, springing up on her toes as if her life was just so buoyant and joyful she could hardly keep from flying. Her over-protective mother had rightly assumed I was trustworthy and placed the care of her precious one in my hands. If her mother knew what went on in our house, if she had any inkling of the images I could have left etched on the soul of her sheltered daughter, she would have never let her near me, nor our house. I endured Elizabeth's endless chatter and her occasional impromptu pirouette on the way to school, so that on the return trip I could run lines with her and hopefully entice her to the garage roof for a "performance" once she finished her three o'clock piano lesson.

After delivering Elizabeth safely to her door I returned home, right on time, nibbling on a peanut butter-coconut ball her mother had pressed upon me. Passing through our living room I noticed first the empty beer cans and then my stepfather, eyes glued to some shoot-em-up western on TV. I tiptoed past him, having witnessed this scenario before. His presence in the middle of the afternoon on a work day meant only one thing. I planned to make myself scarce as soon as I finished my chores. In the kitchen I poured myself a glass of milk to help wash down the gooey ball. My mother was busy tenderizing a cheap piece of meat for dinner, by pounding it to pieces with a butcher knife. I could tell she'd been crying.

"What's wrong, Mom?" I asked, rubbing her back, which seemed to get more boney with each passing year.

She choked back tears, and wiping her forehead with the back of her arm, told me to change clothes and go outside and play. By the time it took me to shimmy out of my school dress, they had started winding up. The volume and sarcasm in their voices was a sure sign that this was going to be a big one. Before I could change, pad downstairs and slip out the back door, the Fiestaware had begun flying, and from her terrified screams I imagined my mother had been punched at least once, maybe twice.

I knew better than to interfere; I had been warned to stay out of their fights. Instead of tiptoeing out the door, like I should have, like I had in the past, I burst through the swinging door and into the kitchen where I found my mother on her knees, being held up by a handful of hair by Tom who was drawing back to give her another punch.

"Stop it!" I yelled. My mother's battered face turned towards me, her lower lip bloody and quivering.

"Get out of here!" he commanded.

As I took a step toward the back door, my mother looked me straight in the eye and said something she had never said before, "Julia, run next door and call the police."

I started to bolt, when he grabbed my shirt from behind and said, with all seriousness, "You call the police and I'll make sure she's dead by the time they get here." I wrenched free from his grasp and turned to my mother for direction.

"Julia, get the police," she said, her eyes flat, expressionless. I nodded.

"I mean it," he said, raising his fist to hit her again.

Everything stopped. The Drink Coca-Cola clock on the wall ticked so loudly I could feel the seconds counting off inside my skull. *Three o'clock. Elizabeth would be lifting her petticoats out behind her as she took a seat at the piano bench.* They both looked at me to see what I'd do. I felt the weight of all families, battered and bruised, settling on me, and it was almost too heavy to bear.

"OK, just don't hurt her, please," I cried, half hysterically. Death in my own kitchen was something that had never occurred to me before that moment. When it came to their fights, there was a sequence: yelling, screaming, hitting, then making up. Always the same. No *death.*

"Get out of here. NO police, you hear me."

"Yes sir," I said, and left my mother to her fate.

"Julia!" my mother cried as the screen door slammed shut behind me. I covered my ears and ran off to the roof of the garage where I invented a play that involved a beautiful girl living happily all alone on a South Seas Island, her only companions being dolphins and whatever fishes swam beside her in the warm water. In my drama the girl spent a lot of time underwater where she couldn't hear anything, certainly no screaming for help.

After awhile there was silence. It was as if the house was deserted, as if they had both disintegrated in their rage. My hands shook as I opened the screen door. The walls were splattered with blood. Fear swept over me and settled in my stomach. I wretched once, running to the sink. There in the sink lay the butcher knife. My heart froze as I surveyed the bright yellow kitchen more closely. The dish drainer and all its contents were on the floor, along with a can of mushroom soup and a frying pan. My only thought was that he *had* actually killed her. I puked again before I went looking for her.

She was not far away. She was lying curled up in a tight ball against the wall, under the kitchen table. I crawled over to her. "Mom. Mommy," I cried, shaking her, trying to get some response. There was none. I rolled her over onto her back. Her face, her beautiful face, was unrecognizable. She had already begun to turn purple and both eyes were well into the process of swelling shut. Her nose looked broken and way too large for her face. Her mouth was slack and a trickle of blood spilled out when I turned her. I screamed.

That brought her to. "Help me to bed," she whispered. I had to drag her, but I'd be damned if I'd ask him for help. Once I got her on to the bed, dabbed some of the blood off her, and placed an ice bag on her head, I went in to confront her attacker.

"She needs to go to the hospital," I said, fists clenched at my side.

"I suppose you're right," he said, taking another swig of beer.

"I think you should drive. I don't know how."

He looked up at me. "You're a smart ass, you know that?"

"Right now I'm a smart ass with a broken mother."

At the hospital I wouldn't leave her side until the doctor convinced me that she wasn't going to die. She was quizzed repeatedly by the hospital staff, "Mrs. Schurr, would you like to press charges?" To which she repeatedly declined the offer.

She would be all right they reassured her. Her nose would have to be reset and she'd be bruised for quite awhile, but her cuts were superficial and would heal without much scarring, if any. They gave her some pills to take once she got home if she had trouble sleeping and slipped her the phone number of an attorney that worked with *these types of cases.* By the time she was ready to be released he had drunk enough coffee to sober up and look remorseful. He wasn't though. We no sooner got her home when he asked, in all seriousness, "What's for dinner?"

By the time Shelly made her debut, Tom's violent behavior had become commonplace. It was, no doubt, fueled by his love for uppers. He'd take just about anything to keep himself hopped up, and when he couldn't get his hands on a particular drug of choice, he'd resort to a poor man's high—he'd eat the Benzedrine-soaked cotton out of nasal inhalers.

I had seen him do this on more than one occasion and never thought too much about it. I just assumed it was some German dietary weirdness. One Saturday afternoon he enlisted my aid. There were only two drugstores in town at that time—a Thrifty and a Beasley's. The first stop was Thrifty's, where I was given a twenty dollar bill and instructed to go in and buy three Benzedrine inhalers. They only had two.

"Do you have any more of these?" I asked the girl behind the counter. She tried to encourage me to try another brand if I had to have three, but I had my instructions—only Benzedrine.

Tom cracked one open and popped the cotton in his mouth the minute I got back to the car. We then drove on to Beasley's. "Try to get another three," he told me. For some reason he kept the car idling as I headed off in search of the inhalers. I found not three, but four of them on the shelf. I knew this would please him so I scooped up all four and handed them to Mr. Beasley, the pharmacist.

"So many?" he said, looking at me over the rim of his wire glasses.

"I can pay for them," I announced, pushing a wad of bills and some coins toward him.

He pushed them back across the counter. "You hang on to that a minute and let's see what we can find over here." He put his hand on my shoulder and steered me back over to the row of decongestants.

"Here's a good one," he said, handing me a Vick's inhaler.

"No, just those, please." I pointed back to the counter that held my bullet-shaped treasures. He took a deep breath, and still holding onto my shoulder, bent down until he was eye-to-eye with me. He didn't say anything at first, just stared at me real hard. I lowered my head and blushed under his scrutiny.

Pointing his finger at me, he said, "You better be careful how you use these. They can be very addictive you know."

"They're for my dad," I whispered, noting that an older girl from my school and her mother were walking down the aisle toward us. I wanted out of there, but I knew I couldn't come back empty handed. He saw the girl and her mother, and ushered me back over to the register.

"What's your dad's name?"

"Tom," I replied. He began writing something down and I knew we were caught.

"Last name?"

"Presley." He clucked twice, put the pen down and wagged his finger at me one last time before he rang up my purchases.

The heat of his stare on my back, I left the store quickly being careful not to run, imagining that it would add to his suspicion. Once back in what I now considered the getaway car I issued the order, "Drive!" Clutching the bag tightly in my lap, staring straight ahead, I pondered a name change—Bonnie, perhaps. He did as I said.

"What happened in there?" he asked as we screeched around the corner of Third and Oleander. A race for home. I told him everything, start to finish, embellishing just a tad on my role.

"Jesus Christ, Julia!" he yelled, hitting the steering wheel with the heel of his hand and rolling his head in disgust. *"Four* of them! You took it upon yourself to draw attention to us by buying *four* of them!" he yelled, red-faced and glaring. "When I specifically told you to buy three!" I wasn't sure what to say, so I said nothing.

"Damn it to hell!" he shouted, hitting the steering wheel again.

"I thought you'd be happy!" I tried. "They only had two at the last store," I held up my fingers to illustrate my point. "Six minus two, leaves four, not three."

He made some kind of growling noise, then got silent, uncharacteristically silent. If it hadn't been for him shaking and banging the steering wheel periodically, I wouldn't have guessed he was still upset. Once home, he snatched the bag off my lap and stomped off into the bedroom yelling for my mom. I went back to washing the dishes that I'd had to leave when he enlisted my services in the drugstore capers. I could hear them yelling through the closed door. Accustomed to the yelling, I had learned to tune it out by singing: "In a pawn shop, on a corner in Pittsburgh, Pennsylvania, I ain't got a thing left to hock . . ."

* * *

**The song brought back a pleasant memory for me.** I was four and Mom and I were having lunch at the Santa Monica Soda Fountain when someone played the song on the jukebox. The combination of my new dress and petticoats, my Shirley Temple ringlets and the fact that I knew all the words to that particular song, were just too much for me. I didn't give it even a moment's thought before I jumped up on the soda counter and started "tap" dancing and singing my heart out to my fellow patrons.

If my mother was surprised when she exited the lady's room to find me entertaining the crowd, she didn't show it. She let me finish my number—which she watched from the back of the room, proud that my performance was being well received—and when it was over she took my hand and announced, "Ladies and Gentlemen, let's hear it for Miss Julia La Chance!" Thankfully, everyone clapped and laughed and thought I was cute. So I curtsied, she lifted me down, and we finished our cokes. It was my first taste of stardom.

I had my hands in the soapy water, searching for missed utensils before I emptied the sink, and had just started the second verse when *'Swock'.* I was hit in the head from behind. I ducked and she hit me again.

"Wait. I didn't . . ." I began to explain.

"Shut up!" she said through clenched teeth. She grabbed me by my shirt, spun me around and pinned me against the kitchen wall, holding me there by grasping great handfuls of my hair. I could see by her face that she had been hit and I knew by previous encounters of this sort, that I was about to become the unwilling recipient of the frustration and anger she held for him. She began by slamming the back of my head into the wall. One slam for each word: "Don't-You-Ever-Disobey-Him-Again." She clutched my hair so hard that later I would pull huge chunks of hair from my brush. She slammed my head into the wall with enough force and repetition to create a whiplash effect that would in later years be the cause of pre-mature arthritic changes in my cervical spine and the source of on-going neck pain and headaches. I never sang that song again.

Why she decided to have another child is beyond me, but she did. Right around the time Shelly joined us, I was one sad little girl. The beatings continued over the most minor of infractions—putting a dish in the wrong place or not folding the laundry correctly. Somehow she had managed to convince herself that if it weren't for me she'd be happily married. There were days I'd walk to school, my legs bleeding from the repeated blows of a switch or one of Tom's belts. She'd lay me over the edge of her bed, pants down to my ankles and flail away until she drew blood.

The bruises and bleeding didn't go unnoticed, however, by the school teachers, nor did they disregard my plummeting grades. More than once they took me aside and tried to convince me to let them summon the police. I protested mightily. People could get killed around our house if the police were ever called. They capitulated and watched in silence, afraid of a time when I wouldn't show up at all. At that point in history the Child Protective Services Agency was not yet formed, and there were no volunteer organizations, like C.A.S.A (Court Appointed Special Advocate) to provide a voice in court for an abused child. Those years had not yet seen the likes of the brave little girl who, with the help of an attorney, would eventually challenge the courts to pull child abuse cases from the jurisdiction of the Society for the Prevention of Cruelty to Animals. In essence, children were considered chattel.

My teacher would personally call our house on days I'd miss school. My instructions were clear; I had a tummy ache, sniffles, a fever. The real reason I stayed home was far more benign than my teacher suspected—I was kept home to babysit my new baby sister. Although I hated missing school, I loved my new sister and delighted in every gurgle and coo. One evening, while my mom entertained the neighbor lady in the kitchen, I was in the bedroom playing with Shelly.

"Oh we ain't got a barrel of money . . ." I sang to her while I changed her wet diaper. By the time we celebrated her making it to the one-month marker, I had mastered her cotton diapers, taking special care they were tight enough to keep her from leaking. That evening, in an attempt to get the diaper nice and snug I pricked her with the diaper pin, which understandably sent her into a howl of protest. Mom came running.

"I didn't mean to . . ." I started to whimper and back out of the room when she grabbed one of Tom's belts. She reared back to get a good swing at me, and in doing so, inadvertently hit Shelly's foot with the buckle. Shelly wailed, and I got the buckle once across the face. She pushed me into the closet to stand in the darkness contemplating my dismal fate, with the admonition, "Don't sit down and don't wrinkle anything."

After an hour or two, the door suddenly opened half way and the neighbor lady reached in, stroked my hair and handed me a chocolate chip cookie. "You're a good girl, Julia," she whispered, "Don't ever forget that," she said, gently closing the door.

When a child is abused, they are likely to grow up disturbed in some way, the pain reaching far into their future waits to claim them at some later date. The ones that mature without any significant damage were fortunate enough to (1) have had a sympathetic adult witness to the abuse. Someone who will step forward, acknowledge the wrong and tell the child "This is wrong and it's not your fault;" and (2) the child has to *get it* that they are not inherently bad and thus deserving of such treatment. Both of these things happened for me that day with that one kind gesture and I was forever changed. I also derived great comfort, henceforth, from chocolate chip cookies.

I realized, standing there amongst the moth balls and spray starch, that somehow through no fault of my own, my life had taken this dreadful turn and it was just a matter of time before I could start creating a life more suitable for myself. I also knew that I would have to keep my wits about me to protect Shelly.

I began focusing on what my life would one day look like. I imagined children laughing and playing on a large grassy lawn while my husband and I sipped ice tea nearby and gazed lovingly into each other's eyes. Naturally the husband I envisioned would be the grown-up version of whatever boy I found particularly cute that week.

* * *

**When I was twelve**, that boy was Brian McNolty. One evening after supper, my hair in rollers, and cotton candy polish drying on my toe nails, I sat on my bed, deep into imagining my future life with Brian. Mom was off visiting a friend and because I had just gotten Shelly down, I had some rare free time for daydreaming. My favorite scene—the one where he reaches across our root beers and cupping my face lovingly in his hands, kisses me—had just begun to roll across my mental movie screen. My recurring response is to burst into song: "Oh Brian, I'll never stop say-ay-ing Brian . . ." to the tune of "Maria" from *West Side Story*. My solo was cut short by Tom, who opened my bedroom door and leaning against the door jam, asked me simply, "Do you like boys yet?"

A simple question, but one I couldn't answer. Tom's sudden interest in my non-existent love life left me flailing about in uncharted waters. I was unaccustomed to heart-to-heart chats with my stepfather and responded to his inquiry by picking at the chenille flower on my bedspread. Tom had never laid a hand on me, leaving that to my mother, but he hadn't shown me any affection either. I was called upon nightly to bestow a goodnight kiss on the cheeks of both parents, regardless of what atrocities had been committed during the day, but other than that, I doubted that we'd had any physical contact whatsoever. So I was, of course, timid when he asked me to give him a back rub.

I was pretty good at back rubs, having practiced for years on my mother, and was proud my expertise. He removed his tee shirt and lying face down on my bed, tucked his hands under his thighs. I straddled him, like I did Mom, and began digging in deep.

"Lower," he instructed. He repeated his command three times until he finally got up and took off his jeans to give me better access.

"There, right there," he said as I rubbed his sacrum. He moaned, then said, "OK, your turn."

"That's OK," I said, jumping up and adjusting my rollers.

"Nope. Lie down."

Reluctantly I layed face down on my pink chenille bedspread, forgetting about my toe polish, my senses alert. I knew something was wrong, but I couldn't tell *what* exactly. Nor did I know what to do. He began rubbing my legs and butt.

"My shoulders are a little tight," I offered, trying to raise up and pointing him away from my bottom.

"Umm," he replied and lowered his body onto mine.

Tom Schurr was twenty-six at the time. He stood five feet and ten inches tall, weighing in at around two hundred pounds. His blood pumped amphetamine through his extremities and he wanted sex. His twelve-year-old stepdaughter who struggled beneath him, had never been kissed, had just started menstruation, and had small apricot-sized breasts was handy. She would do. He stuck his tongue in my ear and started rubbing his fully engorged penis on my behind.

"Don't," I said, turning my head to the other side to escape the wet of his tongue. He reached underneath my nightgown and started pinching my left breast. I jerked around, trying to get away.

"Relax!" he instructed. By that time my curlers were falling out and the side of my head was slick with slobber.

"Please, stop it!" I cried, trying to push him off. He responded by pushing his finger into my vagina. I sobbed, bucked and twisted and tried to yell, but he turned me over and covered my mouth with his hand.

"Shhh. This won't hurt if you relax. You're going to like this. This time next week, you'll be begging me for it." He steered his penis between my legs. I kicked at nothing and yelled into his hand. Tears poured from my eyes and filled both ears. In my mind's eye the root beer glasses shattered, the table broke, and the adult Brian and all our future children, disappeared.

"Julia?! Daddy?!" I heard Shelly cry from the doorway.

"Holy Shit!" he yelled, jumping up and covering himself with his jeans.

* * *

**I was successful** in convincing Shelly that she was sleepwalking and had experienced a bad dream. I curled up next to her, holding her tight, trying not to think about what had just happened. Not an hour went by before he came and knelt at her bed.

"Julia, I'm so sorry," he whispered, so as not to wake Shelly. "I don't know what came over me. Probably the drugs. I'm going to stop, I promise. And I swear to you that nothing like this will ever happen again. I swear it. Please forgive me and above all else don't tell your mother."

I started to sob as silently as I could.

"Promise me, OK? I need you to promise me. If your mother finds out it will *crush her.*"

"OK, I promise," I reluctantly agreed.

"Good girl. Now get some sleep."

When my mother came home around two in the morning she came in to check on Shelly and found me folded up around her sleeping. She shook me, hard, to wake me up.

"What are you doing in here? Get your hands off her. What have you been up to?"

I got up and started to my room when she shoved me through the door. "That baby is not your personal property, you know."

I turned toward her to object, when Tom, for once, came to my defense. "Oh leave the girl alone, will you?"

For as much as I daydreamed about Brian, I would have been disappointed to learn how infrequently, if ever, he thought about me. To be more precise, I wasn't really sure he knew my name. But I knew it was just a matter of time.

As luck would have it, my cousin Linda and her family moved into Brian's subdivision and just down the street from the boy of my dreams. I couldn't wait to pay her a visit.

She called one afternoon when I was knee deep in my daydreams of him.

"He's outside playing basketball with his older brother, who is also pretty cute. We could stroll by. Can you come over?"

"I have to do laundry first. Maybe after."

"I have a new bra."

"What size?"

"Twenty-eight A"

"Oh! I can't wait to see it." I still wore a twenty-eight AA. *"Looks like a band-aid on a bee sting,"* my mother had said.

I washed and pulled the clothes through the ringer, trying to speed up the process. Once they were rinsed, wrung out again and hung on the line to dry, I might have a shot at going. It was a school holiday and no one had thought to tell Beth, the straight-laced, white-haired Jehovah's Witness babysitter she needn't come, an oversight neither of my parents were pleased about. My mom worked at the Piggly Wiggly as a meat wrapper and wouldn't be home until six. Beth would have dinner on the table by then and with any luck, I would have had my first conversation with Brian and made it back before my mother got home from work. I was planning what I'd wear and what I'd say when I would finally be able to speak with him face to face. "Wow, you sure can make those baskets! Can you teach me how to dribble?" *Oh well, something will come to me if I can ever get this laundry out, I bet Tom would let me go.*

"Julia?" I didn't know how long he'd been standing there, or if the monologue I had been running had been all in my head or if I'd actually spoken out loud. Knowing me, the latter was probably the case.

"Yes?" I stayed focused on my chore, the incident that we were never going to mention was still fresh in my mind and I was having a difficult time making eye contact with him. It had been two weeks but I could still smell his breath on my neck.

"Would you like to go to Linda's for the afternoon?"

I was too thrilled for words. Maybe my luck was changing. Maybe he felt so guilty about what he did that he'll spend the rest of his life trying to make it up to me.

I told him I could be ready in about two hours, after I finished the laundry. To my surprise, he informed me that he had made arrangements with Beth to finish up for me, and we could leave right away.

"Yea! Thank you. I'll be down in five minutes, I'm just going to change real fast," I said, squeezing past him as I ran upstairs. "I'll just call Linda to let her know I'm coming!" I yelled down.

"No, don't do that. You'll just show up—surprise her."

I sat in the front seat, as close to the passenger door as I could. He placed a gym bag on the seat between us and off we went. We hadn't gone far when he reached in the bag and pulled out a plastic tupperware tumbler with what Shelly would have called a 'suckee top.'

"Here, I brought you a Coke for the road. Thought you might be thirsty after all that laundry."

"Thanks. Where's yours?"

"I just had a beer. I'm fine. Go ahead. Drink up."

I smiled at his thoughtfulness and took a big drink. It tasted bitter. I pulled off the lid and found white particles floating on top. "There's something in here," I announced.

"Yeah?" he said, surprised. "Let's see." He took the glass. "I see what you mean." He took a small sip. "Tastes OK to me. Go ahead—it'll cool you off."

"No thanks," I said, putting the drink back in the bag.

"Julia, here. Take it," he said, holding out the tumbler.

"No thanks," I repeated, arms crossed for emphasis.

"Julia, c'mon, take it," he said, holding it out in front of me.

I took it, opened the car door and spilled it onto the road that passed by beneath me.

"Why did you do that?" he demanded.

"It was bitter."

He sighed heavily, put the empty tumbler back in the bag, then said, "No problem, just thought you'd like a Coke. That's all."

Having never been to Linda's new home, I had no idea where we were suppose to be going, but I was pretty sure it wasn't up the hill into Willis State Park.

"Do you know where their new place is?" I asked.

"Sure. It's on the other side of the park. We'll just take a short cut here."

Once we were in the park, he drove until we were away from the picnic grounds, the Ferris wheel and the families enjoying themselves on holiday. He pulled to the side of the road, got out, relieved himself in the bushes, then got back in.

"I have something here I'd like to show you," he said, reaching into the gym bag. To my horror, he pulled out *The Green Box.* I knew what was in there. Linda knew too. We had discovered it in the bottom of the linen cabinet one night when she slept over. It had shocked us and filled us with questions. Ultimately it had sent us into fits of girlish giggles. Inside were photos of women with dogs, women with donkeys and three or four of a woman sucking on a man's penis. I had no intention of viewing these photos again in the presence of my stepfather.

He opened the box. "I don't want to see," I said, turning my head to the window.

"But here . . ." I could see by his reflection in my window that he was pawing through the stack trying to find one I might like. ". . . this one will make you laugh."

"I want to go to Linda's."

He fanned the photos out like a poker hand. "Oh, now here's a good one," he said to the back of my head. I remained arms crossed and staring out the window.

"All right, we'll go then. It's not far now. Hey, I have an idea. You drive!"

"Me?" I said turning to face him, thinking he must be crazy. I didn't know how to drive, for God's sake. "I don't think I can."

"Sure you can. You'll do fine. It's automatic. I'll take care of the accelerator, you just sit here in the driver's seat and steer. Easy. Come on."

"OK," I said, my heart racing. This was turning out to be an exciting day after all. Brian *and* driving.

"Here. Slide over the top of me." Reluctantly I did and was relieved that he scooted on over without touching me more than was necessary to make the switch. He pointed toward a narrow road that wound up a hillside. "Just keep your eyes on the road. That's it. Good." I steered toward the road. It was narrow enough to take all my concentration and then some. The road was steep and got windier as we went along. I was pretty proud of myself—driving on such a twisty road. He helped me out by applying just a little pressure to the gas pedal, going slow, making it easier to steer.

Finally, toward the top of the hill, the road straightened out a bit and as we were barely creeping along by that time, I had an opportunity to take my eyes off the road just long enough to see my stepfather masturbating next to me. When he saw my look, he said "Eyes on the road." He put his hand between my legs. My eyes began to fill with tears, not from fear or desperation, but from the humiliation of being stupid enough to have been duped into such a compromising situation. We were in the middle of nowhere and he had no intention of taking me to Linda's. What he intended I could barely imagine, but a particular photo from *The Green Box* sprang to mind, and I felt nauseous.

There was no thought process involved. There was no weighing and considering—no thought of consequences. I stomped down on his foot that rode the gas pedal, simultaneously cutting the wheel toward the left. He yelled and grabbed the wheel two seconds before we plummeted to our deaths off the side of the mountain. We sat in silence balanced at the edge of the cliff. His penis was no longer in sight.

I got out of the front seat and into the back, arms folded, angry more than scared. He put it in reverse and drove us home without another word. The jig was up and he knew it. He dropped me off at the curb outside our house. He knew *sorry* and *don't tell* weren't going to work with me this time. I was telling. That's all there was to it.

I never told my mother, however, never discussed it with her at all. Beth got the story instead. Beth, the lilly-white grandmother of four, got every single detail from the back rub to the cliff. I spared her nothing. She flew into a tizzy, began wringing her hands, pacing and crying. She was so busy being upset, she forgot to comfort me. She phoned my mother at work. When Mom arrived home an hour later, Beth took her off in the bedroom and relayed the details. When they emerged, although my mom's eyes were wet, she couldn't bring herself to look in my direction. Not once.

"Get some clothes together for you and Shelly. We're leaving," was all she said to me. We stayed at Beth's trailer that evening and at Virginia's, my mom's friend, for the next week or so until we moved into our new home, just the three of us.

My mother never asked me about what happened and never offered a hug or any reassurance that everything was going to be all right. I just had to take that one on faith. Even though I only got to tell my story once, I was careful to make it accurate. It felt good to get it all out, every last detail. The fact that some action had been taken left me feeling vindicated. Unfortunately that victorious feeling was short lived.

* * *

**I adored the new house** and had hopes of things returning to what they had once been, now that Tom was out of our lives. I tried to get Mom to sit up with me at night to watch old movies. No go. I propped Shelly up on her bed and encouraged her to make doggie pictures in the dark with the coal of her cigarette, like she had for me many years before, but she didn't have any interest in that or anything else, for that matter. I noticed the medallion she had always worn was missing. We lived in our cute two-story gingerbread house with its picket fence and its roses growing everywhere, for all of three months, before my mother very simply and very clearly told me how it was going to be.

"Your stepfather is coming over for dinner tonight."

My mouth dropped open. I hadn't seen him since that day on the cliff. Had not spoken one word to him since he brought me back from the park and went into hiding at his buddy's house.

"And you are going to greet and welcome him at the door."

I thought I was going to faint from the shock of it, from the betrayal. "I can't," I said, holding on to the back of a chair.

"You will and you'll do it with a smile. I'm sick and tired of you wrecking my marriage. It's your fault I'm separated from my husband, and you're going to try and make it up to me tonight by being pleasant," she said glaring at me. "And if you can't do that, then you'll be the one to leave—not him!"

Unable to stand any longer, I sat down, heavy with the realization that I had lost the mother of my memories. The mother with curls piled atop her head, the mother who drove with the top down singing songs at the top of her voice, the I-Want-To-Get-Married mother, that doggie-drawing-in-the-night mother was now gone for good. I had a hard time breathing, but I knew what I had to do. I set the dinner table.

I moved through that evening like an automaton. A very essential part of me had left my body there to smile and say all the right things. That very essential part waited at the top of the stairs, holding a baseball bat, silently waiting. When it was all over and I had done the dishes and was excused, they retired to her room and began a noisy evening of lovemaking, while I joined the rest of me waiting at the top of the stairs, where I sat all night with the bat, just in case.

The sixties decade was a joy ride for Tom. The plethora of new drugs that were readily available made him absolutely giddy. He tried everything he could get his hands on, including women, which were also in abundance. He started coming home smelling like Patchouli oil after having been missing for the better part of a week and would give Mom some phony story about being off in Oregon saving redwood trees. At least he came back with gifts. He brought my mom some sandalwood perfume she never would wear, accurately surmising that the scent would remind him of Rainbow, the hippie chick he spent hours talking to on the phone. Shelly got a cute little shammie shirt embroidered with beads and hung with feathers, which she loved and wanted to sleep in every night. I got love beads, which were never worn and were thrown to the back of the top shelf of my closet.

The best part of the sixties for me was that it mellowed him out a bit. It was hard for him to walk around flashing the peace sign at everyone while he was pummeling his wife at home. He grew pot in the backyard, which was a never-ending source of anxiety for my mother. She tried everything she could think of to kill it, but it was hearty and kept coming back. One day a police officer showed up at the door and it sent her into a tailspin. She hid in her room, making me answer the door. The officer was in the neighborhood that day going from door to door in an attempt to raise money for the Police Officer Fund for After School Athletics. Once he was safely out of sight, my mother went out and uprooted what was left of Tom's marijuana plants, brought them in the house, chopped them up and served them to him for dinner that night, stir-fried, over brown rice. That was it for Tom. Once he came down he packed his bags and left us, "for good," he claimed. *For good,* I prayed.

So once again it was the three of us. In that the sixties hadn't done anything to temper my mother's anger and cruelty, I had little expectations as to any sudden conversion once he was gone. I knew by then that she was not cut out for motherhood. In fact, she had become more mean-spirited and cruel with each passing year. Still, with any change in my environment, came hope. I looked for signs of change everywhere. I even looked for it in its more subtle guises, the shifting hues at the turning of day to night, or the welcoming slide to minor notes within a melody. Change came to be synonymous with reprieve, a dropped stitch in the day-to-day fabric of a tattered life.

* * *

**When girlfriends came by** to visit Mom, they always gathered in our kitchen. I kept their coffee cups filled and ashtrays emptied in an attempt to hold them there. My sister had her own, more direct methods, which ranged from impromptu singing to literally throwing herself on the woman and begging her not to leave. The reason for this display was simple. Mom would change into a different person when she had company, and I could catch glimpses here and there of the mother I remembered from when I lived with Nana. She'd toss her head back and laugh freely and tell funny stories. She was delightful and charming. It was these moments that perplexed me most. I couldn't understand how it was possible for her to live her daily life as a tyrant, when she had such a beautiful person locked up inside her. I'd listen to their conversation from around the corner in the hall, trying to find something in her laughter that I could hold on to, something that would justify the love I had once felt for her.

I liked to fantasize that this entertaining, laughing woman who filled the kitchen with smoke from her cigarettes was my real mother and that the last nine years had been spent with an imposter. Now that she was back, in her new, improved version, things would be better. If laundry products could metamorphose into new and improved versions of their former selves, *why not mothers?* My desire was so strong that at times I could almost manage to convince myself that a miracle had taken place. As I entered the kitchen, Marilyn, her friend, would smile at me over her coffee cup, her brown eyes warm and welcoming. I'd smile back, and in an attempt to please, would start drying the racked dishes and putting them away. I'll admit, I was also secretly enjoying the new warmth of the kitchen, due to the miracle that had just taken place in my imagination.

The comradery of the two women made me feel somehow safe. It was there that I came to learn the value of women friends and I wanted to bask in the powerful glow that surrounded them as they enjoyed each other's company. Amber streaks of light cut through the smoky haze of the kitchen aiming right at their small table, as if blessed from on high. At the kitchen sink, my back to the table, the sound of their voices, one husky, one soprano, danced around me carrying me to greater heights of illusion. I took my time drying the plates, feeling and sensing the textures of the moment. I was willing to suspend belief in all things past, if only I could have a life filled with moments such as these. I felt connected to women everywhere who cooked, dried their dishes, and met in small kitchens to smoke and laugh together.

I remembered with great fondness the time I had spent in the kitchen with Nana, stirring pots and chattering away, her listening intently to my childish ramblings. I missed her. Mom had no more use for her once Baba died, and although I had only managed to see her a couple of times since, she never forgot my birthday and there was always something for me and Shelly at Christmas time.

"Right back," I heard Marilyn announce. A chair pushed back, wooden chair on tile floor—a scraping sound. I turned to offer a smile as if she was addressing the two of us. I caught my mother's eye instead. Her rheumy glare shocked me back to reality. Her lip would have curled in disgust if it hadn't been held in place by the Pall Mall. "Get out," she said slowly, and with deliberate malice. Her voice was low and heavy, the weight of it found its way to the bottom of my heart where tears are stored. I could feel the hatred in her eyes follow me out of the room. She lifted her head and exhaled forcefully. I knew then that she wanted to blow me out of the room and out of her world. I also knew that those feeling were not just for me. She would have blown Shelly away too if she could. I imagined Shelly tumbling through the air on cigarette breath as I walked stiffly across the hall and into her room. She was safe, playing alone on the floor with her dolls. Shoe boxes, ashtrays, tiny cups and saucers surrounded her, creating a makeshift doll's world.

She scanned my face for clues, trying to ascertain the climate of the moment. With the slightest nudge from me, she was prepared to jump up, leave her plastic children and melt into the walls if that's what it took to avoid the next anticipated onslaught. I hid from her. There were no tears. I saved tears for the big things.

Relieved at my smile, she returned to dollworld. "Julia? Which do you like better? This?" she asked holding up a small lump of fabric, "or this?"

All I saw and felt was color. "The red," I managed to say, before I turned and left the room.

I entered my senior year in high school counting the days until I could leave and start making a real life for myself. I had stopped participating in the after school activities that I loved, such as Drama Club, because although I was a natural at acting—every day was an act for me at home—I couldn't make it to rehearsals. Mom thought that if I had time to sit down and read a book or a script, then I had time to wash windows or whatever chore she could pass from her shoulders to mine. I loved school and wanted to do well, but my views were not shared by my mother who lumped homework into a category she considered free time. And free time was something she was intent on using to her own advantage.

My art teacher insisted I had talent. She called my slapdab watercolor of Shelly inspired. I was inspired all right, inspired to find beauty and inspired to escape into it. I loved the way the colors first mingled and eventually fused with each other. I yielded to the translucence and the illusion of depth. I discovered that if I rubbed an aquamarine between my fingers I would find the ocean there. The shapes I painted were secondary to the trail of color that I traveled with my brush. And I traveled far, transformed by the textures, the play of light across a canvas, the vestige of turpentine on my skin that followed me home, a reminder of beauty. A promise. Eventually I found my way into the darkroom and discovered why God created the planet. Bending over the enlarger, burning and dodging images onto paper, satisfied some primal urge to express myself. And then to watch the developer tray—closely, poised to yank my creations should they dare to become too brazen, too bold—in the shy red of the room, as they were born in their own cosmic soup, lifted me out of my life and stood me alongside others who dared to shape their world in clay, in color and in light.

* * *

**I was studying for midterms** one Sunday morning when Mom called me into the bathroom to help her with her hair. It's hard to come to terms with the aging process, regardless of who you are and how you've lived your life, but it's doubly frustrating for a woman like my mother who had gotten by on her looks, to bear witness to the slow collapse of collagen and the other dirty tricks nature plays on women who have outlived their childbearing usefulness.

"See that flat spot right there?" she said, holding a hand mirror and pointing an accusatory finger at the spot in question.

I leaned in, squinting in concern to please her.

"It's right here, look."

"Yep, I think you're right," I said nodding and frowning at the bathroom mirror.

"Pick it out," she commanded. She handed me a pink plastic hair pick and twisted her torso into a contorted knot where, if I stood just-so, I could reach the offending spot and she could still watch to be sure I was doing it correctly. She was nervous. She'd been working on herself for two hours already and was still unable to recapture her former beauty. She was preparing herself for her weekly date at San Quentin. Her friend Marilyn had gotten her started with all this, saying that these inmates really were trying to rehabilitate and a little female companionship did wonders to lift their spirits and help them on their way to becoming better citizens. Naturally, within a matter of months, Marilyn had found the man of her dreams locked within those walls and after a six-month "courtship" had decided to marry the jailbird. They were allowed weekly conjugal visits, now that they were married, which she described to Nora in great detail.

Not to be outdone, Mom had found herself a boyfriend there too. She began dabbing Erase on the varicosities of her right leg.

"Aren't you going to be wearing nylons?" I asked.

"Of course," she replied as she scrutinized the result in the full-length mirror. She had always been proud of her legs and wouldn't miss an opportunity to show them off to their best advantage. The five-inch heels in the corner were polished and ready to go. She, on the other hand, would not be ready for another hour, bringing the entire morning preparations to a full three hours. That meant she would be a good forty-five minutes late. She didn't care. He could wait. Where else did he have to go anyway? Nowhere. Who else was he expecting? No one. For one San Quentin inmate named Lucky, Nora Schurr was the main attraction, the hot tamale, and she knew it.

The stack of letters she kept in her top dresser drawer had now overflowed to include the larger second bureau drawer as well. In these letters that arrived almost daily, Lucky professed not only his undying love for her, but his amazement and appreciation of her beauty. In his eyes she still possessed her *starlet* quality. She wasn't one to disappoint. She darkened the beauty spot on her left cheek, applied a final dab of concealer under both lower lids, neatly folded three squares of Kleenex, which she placed in her new matching handbag, and finally she was ready to go knock'em dead up at Quentin. If she didn't get at least a smattering of cat calls as she walked into the visitor's area she was disappointed, and so was Lucky.

"How do I look?" she said striking a Betty Grable pose.

"Great. You look just great Mom."

"Really?" She checked herself from all sides in the full-length mirror.

"Yeah," I said, with a little less enthusiasm than she felt she deserved. She gave me a critical look then started enumerating my chores for the day, which included nothing less than a complete overhaul of the garden. My day was shot.

"Can it wait until after school tomorrow? I have so much homework to get caught up on," I said, feeling defeated before the battle had even started.

"No, it can't wait. I intend to plant tomorrow and I need it done today."

"But I really need the time. Shorthand class is killing me," I whined, "I can barely make sense of these stupid squiqqles and tomorrow is midterms. I need the time to study." A little too much despair crept into my voice; I had to make her understand.

"Well, now," she said, hands on hips, "If you're going to whine like a baby, then you're going to be treated like a baby. And you know what that means, don't you?"

"Yes, Mam," I said. *Yes, Spam.* I knew all right and it was the one thing that she had threatened me with in recent years that made the hair stand up on the back of my neck. Once she figured out that smashing my head into the wall and kicking me around the room were no longer having much effect on me, she fished around until she found the one thing that would keep me under her thumb. And that one thing was humiliation. Her latest threat was this: She intended to strip me naked, clothe me in diapers, put my hair in a ponytail topknot like Pebbles on the Flintstones, and sit me out on the front yard in Shelly's old play pen, so that in the morning, when all the other high school students were parading by our house on their way to class, they could all witness Julia the whiner.

"So, get the play pen out of the garage and set it up on the front lawn. That's where you'll be tomorrow morning," she said, like it was the most natural thing in the world. "That's what you get for talking back to me and for acting like a baby." She turned to leave, in her five-inch heels, and I was inordinately delighted to see an undetected run in her stocking snaking its way up the back of her calf. I watched as she pulled out of the driveway, and prayed for an accident on the Golden Gate Bridge; maybe while she checked her makeup in the rear-view mirror.

I was seventeen, and six months away from graduating high school. I had stuck it out this long, so naturally I thought I could stick it out until graduation, but this was just too much. I knew I was play pen bound regardless if I did the yard work or not. She was thirty-six and sat at the head of the table. Since the day her husband molested me, she saw me with different eyes, a rival of sorts. The clock was not our ally. Just as gray hairs, wrinkles and booze were staking their claim to her life, I was becoming more a woman. The more visible I became in the world, the less tangible she felt. I had begun to turn heads and she couldn't get a rise out of the garbage man. She should have been in her prime, but fate had caught up with her.

For the last time, I stepped into her bedroom. Her room was a true representation of her current obsession—Lucky, the convict. She had confided in me in a conspiratorial tone one day as I helped her get ready for her *date* with him, that Lucky was innocent and had been left to the mercy of a bad lawyer. The entire trial had been rigged. Scattered across her bed were law books. *A pre-law student preparing for exams.* She had been studying and was almost certain she had found a loophole that would set him free. I knew that in her fantasies she saw herself triumphant before the courts, the darling of the San Quentin set, a convict's Mother Teresa and wet dream all rolled into one. We had never discussed his crime, but I knew theft was at least part of it. I flipped open several of the books to one earmarked passage after another, all dealing with Grand Theft. Theft of what, I couldn't tell you. I didn't have enough curiosity to read further. A crook is a crook in my book.

I looked around the room. In a corner by the window, resting on an orange paper mache' box—a recent craft project—sat the only record player we owned, the kind with a turntable, three speeds and a cylindrical adapter for the donut hole of forty-fives. "Fire and Rain," by James Taylor sat motionless on the player. I considered the melancholy lyrics of the song and tried to imagine what memories might be triggered for her when she played it over and over, as she was prone to do. I wondered which sweet dreams and flying machines she had left in pieces on the ground. I picked up one of her slips that she had left on the bed in the tangle of bed clothes. I breathed her in, trying to find something there that smelled like home, that felt like love. I either didn't have the right receptors or it just wasn't there.

My eyes landed on a photo of myself that she had placed atop her dresser next to a recent one of Shelly. It had been there for some time and I wondered what it was about that particular photo, that particular vision of me, that made me hers. I studied the face. It was a school photo, taken when I was eleven, still gangly, naive, fresh. I wore an intent expression, head cocked slightly to the side, as if trying to understand some instruction given. I wore my plaid dress, the black velvet bow perched lopsided on my flat chest, my breasts yet to be dreamed of or even imagined.

"Goodbye Mom," I said as I closed the door to her room.

* * *

**I took Shelly for a walk,** explaining that I was going away. She stopped dead in her tracks and looked up at me in disbelief. I knelt down and wrapped her limp arms around my neck. "I'm sorry Shell," I said into her hair. "I'll always love you and I promise to come for you as soon as I can."

"Julia, please. You can't go," she said between sobs. "Who's going to look after me? Julia, don't go." Her grandmother Schurr was a kind woman and had always had a soft spot for Shelly. I told her to contact her if she needed help. I pried her arms off, stood up and kissed the top of her head. I wasn't sure if I'd ever to be able to make good on my promise to her and that hurt even more than leaving her crying in the street. I left her standing in front of her friend Carol's house and walked the fifteen blocks to the Pacifica Police Station. On the way there I took an opportunity to drink in the sights and smells of freedom. The ocean was wild that day and windy as usual. I let it blow through me; through the holes that had been left behind by cruelty. I wondered if I would find love, if it truly existed, or if humans were just too selfish to ever care enough for one another. If my own mother couldn't love me, then who could? I would have to wait to learn the answer to that question.

I walked into the Police Station and presented myself to the first officer I encountered.

"Excuse me Sir, but if you have time will you please take me to Juvenile Hall?"

I was determined, when I turned myself over to the police that day, to spend the rest of my seventeenth year under the protection of the juvenile authorities. I figured that once I turned eighteen I would be free to go and would do so, not looking back, but heading toward the bright future that I had envisioned for myself since that day, age ten, when I stood in my mother's closet nibbling a chocolate chip cookie.

The police officers were dumbfounded, having never seen or heard of a child presenting herself in this fashion. They tried to ascertain the problem, offering to speak with my parents to try to bridge the generational gap that they imagined had motivated my decision. I refused to cooperate, the only information I would give anyone until I was safe behind bars was my first name and the fact that I was a runaway. After numerous failed attempts to extract anything pertinent from me, they relented. "Would you like to stop for an ice cream before we get there?" they asked.

I refused their kind offer and took my seat in the back of the squad car. It was a forty-minute drive to my new home. Along the way I distracted myself by watching the scenery change from familiar to foreign. I imagined myself, age eighteen and sprung free: living in that apartment building right there, perhaps working as a secretary for that company that openly recruited on a passing billboard, shopping in that mall. The possibilities were endless. Before I bubbled over with excitement at the prospects, a kernel of doubt crept in and began to grow in my gut until it had grown large enough to be recognized as fear. The only stories I had heard of Juvenile Hall were not pretty. Suddenly I imagined that I might be trading in one form of abuse for another of which I was unfamiliar. At least at home I knew what to expect. I began to tremble and doubt my decision. Fear struck again when I imagined my mother's reaction, her collecting me at my county haven, and what would happen to me once she got me home. That particular mental image made me gasp aloud. The police officer turned to me and said, "You OK?"

"Do you think we could stop for a bag of chocolate chip cookies?" Comfort food might be all the comfort I could get for awhile.

Truthfully, when all was said and done, I had no way of knowing what to expect behind those walls, and although I was accustomed to violent behavior at home, I was not expecting to be met with the level of hostility I encountered from the other girls. New Juvies were the topic of the day amongst the other girls. Until they found out who she was and what she was in for, they didn't know how to react to a newcomer; they weren't sure where she'd fall in the pecking order. So the new girl would be goaded and proded until she reacted. The extent of her reaction, coupled with the label of her crime or misdeed, determined the level of respect she was afforded. Needless to say, a runaway was as low on the pecking pole as one could get, that is if you didn't count a runaway who volunteered her way into Juvenile Hall.

It would get worse for me once they saw that I had no desire to leave. While they sat talking about when they would get out and boasting about what they would do when that glorious day finally came, I'd sit off by myself, humming tunes and reading everything I could get my hands on, content to at last have a little free time.

It didn't help that I obviously enjoyed attending the classes we were required to attend. As far as the other girls were concerned, school was a waste of their precious time; time better spent writing letters to their boyfriends or watching TV. It didn't take much effort to throw that grade curve. Suddenly I was a straight-A student. The girls sneered and called me the runaway brainiac, but I was finding that although I didn't much like the label, I did like the attention I was getting from the teachers. I'd dream up questions for them, so that I could stay after class. They were unaccustomed to having inquisitive students and indulged me. I discovered that more than anything I enjoyed discussions of a philosophical nature. Soon the teachers were entrusting me with books from their home libraries. While the other girls bitched about their one chore of the day, I mopped or swept or dusted the room to which I was assigned and imagined I was enjoying a day at the spa. The more I endeared myself to the house guards, the more it irked my fellow inmates. By the end of the second week of my incarceration they had tired of my chirpy attitude, and let me know about it at every opportunity. I knew I was suppose to be suffering in there with the rest of them, but I just couldn't muster up an adequate display of dissatisfaction to please them. I didn't find it all that bad actually. We had popcorn and movies every Friday night. Wednesday was crafts, which were a bit too basic for my tastes, but it gave me some form of creative outlet, and Thursdays we met individually with a counselor.

I was a little perturbed that no one came to see me on visitor's day, not that I wanted my mom to come, but it would have been nice if someone had brought Shelly to see me. I missed her. I thought for sure Nana would show up, maybe even try to claim me, but she didn't. I found out later that Mom had blocked me from having visitors or any contact with anyone I knew from the outside. No letters, no calls, no nothing. In her book if I wanted to live there, fine, but it was going to be without the sympathy of family and friends. By the end of my sixth week at the Hall, one of the counselors made the mistake of holding me up as an example to the other girls, right before our Friday night movie. Meant of course as encouragement to the other girls, it just caused them to resent me further. I could feel the temperature rise in the room as they shot me heated glances. That was when the trouble really started for me. After that they couldn't stop picking on me, stealing my things, and basically trying to make my life miserable. The staff could see what was going on and began encouraging me to go home. I, of course, refused. Their dislike for me—"*you're just tooo good, aren't you?*"—escalated to the point where I began breaking out in red blotches from the stress, a visible sign they were getting to me. That encouraged them. It didn't take long before they started pushing me around. One girl falsely accused me of using her lipstick and took the opportunity to knock me to the floor over it. My counselor could see what was going on and had me placed in a cell by myself to try to protect me, but that only made things worse. I was further isolated, singled out and they hated the sight of me.

The tension became unbearable. They began threatening me, under their breath, while in the lunch line. I had learned by then not to report such things and tried to suffer through it in silence. My body had other ideas. I woke up one night in a cold sweat, unable to move. It was as if my body had forgotten how to function, or someone had cut the wires that ran from my brain to my arms and legs. Try as I might I was all but rigid. The doctor checked me out thoroughly and pronounced me physically healthy. "So why can't I move?" I asked after the second day of paralysis. He explained that it was my body's defense to stress, something called Neurasthenic Hysterical Paralysis. I was hysterical alright. The staff tried again to get me to go home. Again I refused.

By the third day my body had started functioning again, but the word around the Hall was that I was a girl that just didn't belong in there and that the place was doing me more harm than good. My counselor, Miss Burroughs, came up with a plan. She called me to her office and presented me with a No. 2 pencil and a packet. I passed the G.E.D. with flying colors. She didn't stop there. She and two of my teachers petitioned the court, and four months before my eighteenth birthday, I was bestowed with the status of Emancipated Minor. Through a special State program designed to give worthy candidates a clean start, I was offered a job in the secretarial pool at Hills Brothers Coffee in San Francisco. I would be making four hundred dollar a month to start, with a salary review in six months. I was astounded at my good fortune. But even more than that, I was amazed that someone cared enough to go to bat for me. I was probably the only girl in the history of that institution who cried when she left. My gratitude to Miss Burroughs spilled over onto her silk blouse as I hugged her goodbye.

My other angel, Nana, who had been working behind the scenes all along with Miss Burroughs, was waiting for me when I was given back the clothes in which I had come. Although she was not Loretta Young, and although we had little contact with her after Baba died, she nonetheless cared enough for me to help me out in my time of need. She was livid that my mother had kept her from me all those years and took great satisfaction in extricating me from my current situation.

Nana gave me the boost I needed to insure my independence. At the time, she was living with her new husband in the little flower field called Lompoc, some six hours south of San Francisco. To help me out, she had taken a hotel room not far from where I would be working, so that she and I could scout out an efficiency apartment that I would be able to afford on my new salary. We took long walks together through the streets of San Francisco as we searched for just the right place and I became accustomed to the lay of the land. It took us a week to find my first apartment on California and Buchanan. The rent was one hundred twenty-five dollars a month, leaving me plenty left over for whatever extravagances I could dream up. She was kind enough to loan me the first month's rent and bought me towels and sheets and silverware, which she labeled "a housewarming gift."

During that week, as we explored the city, shopped for sheets and lunched in little smokey cafes, we were able to get re-acquainted and re-establish the bond we had once known when I was a little girl, and she, having never had children, had considered me her own. She asked about my life with Nora, and although I had the desire to unburden myself, I didn't want to do it at her expense. I could feel her sensitivity to such topics and furthermore, I didn't want to change the tone of our time together. I wanted to feel that comradery that I had imagined years ago in my mother's kitchen, where two women could sit together, sharing stories, sipping tea while they bathed in the warmth of each other's companionship. I told her just enough for her to understand why I had no desire to ever see my mother again.

Too soon it was time for her to return home. Although I would miss her, I was grateful to know that I had someone in my life that cared about me, someone I could call, who would be happy for any good that might come my way. Left alone in my new apartment, I wandered the three large rooms, arranging the towels on the rack, re-arranging the silverware in the drawer, fawning over the plastic dishes. I pulled the Murphy bed down from the wall in the living room. I made the bed and had a seat dead center, legs crossed. Taking a quick mental survey of my life up to that point, I made a solemn pledge that now that I was in charge of my life, things would be different.

From that vantage point I could see out past my postage-stamp balcony to California Street. I could hear the cars go by. I knew that two blocks away was a beautiful park where I would spend my leisure time, and that if I stood on the corner of California and Mason, I could catch the cable car to work. I sat on my bed and wondered at the beauty of life that began right there in the spot where I sat and extended out to the streets of San Francisco and beyond, way beyond. I vowed to see as much of the world as my time on the planet would allow. To my surprise, I realized that a part of me believed there were people out there who loved one another and treated each other with kindness and consideration. I was determined to find them.

Liberation day had finally come. I would now make my own choices and live with the consequences of my actions, not the whims of another. Life felt orderly and clean. I felt like Eve before the snake; the first woman to explore the garden. A spark of freedom ran through me like a silver thread that began at the top of my head and made its way slowly down the length of my body. When it finally reached my feet, I just had to dance.

## *Paula:*

I took a few deep breaths. I was still rattled from having bumped into Nora on the Oncology floor. The shock of seeing her mingled uneasily with my anticipation of finally seeing Julia again after such a long time. Visions of Julia's treatment at the hand of Nora continued to spring to mind unsolicited, crashing into one another. My heart began to race. My face felt flushed. Suddenly the elevator felt confined and devoid of sufficient oxygen. I realized I was hyperventilating. I also realized I had to find my composure, for I was about to meet with a client who needed me whole and focused. Thankfully the elevator stopped and I walked straight to the ladies room where I talked myself down, steadied my breathing and ran cool water over both wrists. After about five minutes, I donned my therapist's hat and resumed my search for Felicia's room.

* * *

**She was in better shape than I had hoped to imagine.** My arrival at the hospital preceded her husband's by two hours—he was flying in from Seattle—giving me an opportunity to hear her story and ascertain the current status of her mental health, minus the histrionic rendition she was sure to give her unsuspecting husband. I entered her room quietly, apprehensively, not sure what to expect. She was propped up in bed, her head turned toward the window. She was quiet, not fidgeting as usual, her arms at her sides. I could see that she had lost a nail. With her discriminating fashion sense and flamboyance, the cotton gown held on by frayed strings tied loosely at her neck were incongruous. Overall she appeared limp and vulnerable. The blackness of the night turned her window into a mirror. Once she registered my reflection, she turned toward me.

In spite of the bruises and the tears that ran silently down her cheeks, she managed a twitch of a smile, and a hand gesture that I interpreted as: Come here, sit down. I took a seat beside her, and reached for her hand. "I'm sorry, Felicia," was all I could think of to say at the moment. Without missing a beat she launched into her tale as if she were on the clock. I could see that in her mind the fifty-minute hour had begun. As her story unfolded, I noted that her typical enthusiastic recounting of her *adventure* was absent. More than anything, she appeared remorseful, realizing perhaps for the first time the vulnerable and dangerous situation into which she had willingly placed herself. I considered this a good sign.

She had met him at the Academy of Sciences in San Francisco where, after coquettishly following each other around for an hour, they had finally struck up a conversation about the clown fish nestled in the anemones at Steinhardt Aquarium. This of course had flowed into more conversation over coffee at a nearby Starbucks, which just happened to be a few blocks from his apartment, and lo-and-behold, his brand new aquarium, which he was just dying to show off to someone. Felicia volunteered to be that very someone.

They'd done it on the couch and then again on the floor of the living room—at twenty-three he recovered quickly—and were ready to go a third time when his roommate came in. Felicia, sitting buck naked on his lap, tried to cover herself by throwing her arms around the young man, her backside turned toward the Filipino boy who'd just entered the room. By the barbs they'd slung at one another, it didn't take her long to figure out that she had disrupted a happy little lovenest and the Filipino boy wanted his turn as well, to even the score so to speak. The end result was that her *lover* held her down while his lover had at her virginal ass.

By the time it was over, she had been slapped around a bit, not hard, but enough for her right eye to begin swelling and discoloring. When they were through with her, she was too shaken—*hysterical* the admitting nurse had said—to drive all the way home to Healdsburg and had instead made her way to St. Mary's, where they had admitted and sedated her while they sized up her injuries. Although they hadn't turned up any appreciable physical injuries, they decided to keep her overnight for observation. They intended to release her by noon the next day, after the rape crisis counselor had an opportunity to speak with her. As her therapist, I could have had her released into my care, allowing her to bypass the counselor altogether, but I decided it would be in her best interest to capitalize on the remorse she was feeling and let her lie there for the night reflecting on her actions. I wanted her to fully appreciate how dangerous her lifestyle had become. I explained to Felicia that Charlotte, my replacement, would be following up with her on Monday and that I would be leaving my mobile number and a note for the rape counselor in her chart. Thankfully she seemed fine with that, making it easier for me to stick to my original departure date.

We were in the midst of our farewells when her husband arrived. He came rushing to her side, frightened and concerned. "Oh Charles, it was just horrible . . ." I left as she began her tale. I knew her well enough to know for a fact that the version she'd been telling me would not resemble the story that Charles Welton would hear. I made a mental note that, when I returned, we were going to have to deal with her inability to be honest with her husband.

* * *

**The following day was uneventful**, a short day at the office. I was on the road by lunchtime. I chose Highway 101 over Highway 1, in that it is just too slow for my taste, regardless of its scenic wonders. And I decided against Hwy 5, although it is the fastest of the three routes linking northern to southern California, due to the fact that it's too tedious, with mile after mile of unbroken straight-ahead desolate road. I almost always get a speeding ticket when I take Hwy 5, the boredom settling in the foot that controls the gas pedal. The other thing about that stretch of road that's hard for me to stomach are the cows of the Hartford Ranch. I can't stand to see them, hundreds of them, miles of them, all bunched together in that barren landscape next to the highway with nothing to do, nowhere to walk and nothing to eat except the grain and hay products brought around by ranch employees twice a day. All this to juice them up, make them tastier—the Kobe beef of California.

I've been a vegetarian for many years now. It started with veal and soon included every source of animal protein that has legs and bears its young. Fish are exempt, which is lucky, I'd have a hard time giving up sushi. My diet changed the day Julia discovered a new bike trail. Although she loved to cycle, she hated traffic and was always on the lookout for routes and trails that were used primarily by non-motorized vehicles. It was a great trail, running from Cotati, through Santa Rosa and ending in Sebastopol. We only used it once, however. Just before we reached Sebastopol, we were stopped dead in our tracks by a pitiful sound. On a ranch that ran alongside the trail, a little calf was chained inside a wooded structure just big enough for him to stand up, not big enough for him to turn around, or even scratch. His only view of the world was through an opening large enough for his head to poke out. He was only about fifteen feet off the trail. Close enough for him to reach out and touch my heart.

"What's this?" I demanded of Julia.

"That, Paula," Julia had informed me, "is veal." I'd had sausage that morning before our ride and I could feel it sitting heavily in my belly, suddenly making me want to wretch. I have been a vegetarian ever since.

My conversion, which Julia applauded, spawned our nightly cooking sessions, which I hold partially responsible for sealing our lifelong friendship. We met in my sophomore year at Sonoma State College. She was a year ahead of me, a Fine Arts major. I was undecided about my major and undecided about life in general. At that point in time, my life had been pretty sheltered. I had yet to hold my first job and was unaware of the types of responsibilities she had been forced to shoulder. My parents paid for everything. Julia got by on FISL loans and whatever scholarships she could get her hands on. She worked in a frame shop after class to make ends meet, and occasionally waited tables on weekends or whenever the Changing Hands Café needed her.

She held the lease on a two-bedroom farmhouse out on Pepper Road. It was spacious, furnished with an eclectic mix of bean bag chairs, cinder block bookcases, madras bedspreads and ferns. Perfect decor for young college girls in the early '70's. It was exactly what I had been looking for. It even had a garden. I didn't realize it at the time, but Julia was the friend I was looking for too.

When I first moved in, she had been rather quiet. Not shy exactly, nor was she aloof. She just wasn't chatty like the other girls I had called friend. But she listened well and our bond began to grow over the nightly dinners we made together. As we chopped, diced and stirred, I found myself sharing intimate details of my life, my hopes and my concerns. Somehow it just felt natural while peeling potatoes or seasoning a casserole to tell her these things. Her responses were thoughtful and measured, and I could tell that, for the first time in my life, I was not being judged.

When she gave advice, I was always eager to implement her suggestions, although I never really got the expected result. Probably because, although her advice was sound, it usually required a certain level of detachment to the outcome, which I couldn't quite master. "It is what it is," I'd heard her say on more than one occasion. I finally came to realize that Julia's solutions worked for Julia and would inevitably carry her into an adventure of one sort or another. I would have to find my own answers. That didn't stop me from dressing the dinner table nightly with my problems, however. Eventually she opened her heart to me too.

The patterns of her life began to take shape through the startling and colorful stories she told. At first I thought she was prone to exaggeration, until I came to realize that her life needed no extra flourishes to make it entertaining, and in those rare moments when she reached back to touch the fire of her childhood, excruciatingly painful. It became clear as she felt more free to discuss her childhood that she had managed through determination and a good attitude to move herself through a life that looked like a seamless segway from *Mommy Dearest* to *The Sound of Music.* For her the glass was always half full—never mind that it may be cracked and dirty—it is what it is. She was the poster child for making lemonade from lemons. A fact that didn't always endear her to the more cynical types.

Being around her was just this side of magical. We'd be driving along and she'd be singing a song. At some point, she'd flip on the radio and that very song would be playing on the radio, and more than once at the very same *spot* in the song. She never commented about it, just kept on singing like it was the most natural thing. Or, we'd be walking down the street and she'd say: "My experience has been that tall redheads have the largest penises." Naturally, as we turned the corner, we'd bump into a tall redhead. Fully clothed, of course, but one could imagine. It was non-stop. It was as if she understood some fundamental law of nature that the rest of her friends couldn't quite grasp. Nor could she tolerate whiners. She'd say: "Yes, I see your problem," cutting them off in the middle of their tale of woe, with a coach's time-out hand signal, "here's what you do." She'd go on to explain that thoughts are magnets and wherever you place your focus is what life brings you. Nice words, but nonetheless not always what the whiner wanted to hear, when what she really wanted to do was rip out the carotids of her two-timing boyfriend.

I could never quite pin her down as to her philosophical roots. She was part Objectivist, part Mystic. The more I learned of her early years, the harder it was for me to reconcile what I knew her life must have been like with her current philosophy. It puzzled me how anyone could have made that great a leap from abused child to the well-adjusted, carefree young woman that she had become. It would be some time before I understood the fragile core she guarded, and just how vulnerable she is in certain situations.

By the time her graduation rolled around we were inseparable. So it stood to reason that the day she and I split up our household was a difficult one for both of us. I had a year of undergrad yet to complete, and as she was heading down to L.A. to attend the Art Academy, I decided to try living on my own. I had rented a guest house in Rohnert Park, to be closer to campus, and had moved my belongings to my new place the week of her departure.

As fate would have it, her student loan didn't come in as expected to enable her to pay tuition, a detail overlooked by the financial aid officer until a mere five days before she was scheduled to leave. She was not to be deterred. She sold her van to a friend for the $500 tuition money she needed, bought herself a bus ticket, and proceeded to give away the household possessions she had intended to take with her. People fluttered about the house that weekend, taking with them dishes, plants, an ironing board, a pot or a pan. They made an attempt at small talk but basically left quickly, a little guilty after loading up their cars with her belongings. They knew they were leaving her with nothing and they felt a little like vultures, giving nothing in return. But, after all, they reasoned, they might never see her again and they really did need that vacuum cleaner. They left before she could change her mind.

By Sunday afternoon they had pretty well stripped the place. We sat together on her sleeping bag in the middle of the living room. A seen-better-days overstuffed chair she had snagged at a garage sale the year before stayed behind for the next tenant, as did a potted plant over in the corner by the window. Too large and overgrown to be easily transported, it had not been claimed, so by virtue of its size, it was destined to remain behind with the chair. I gave her a going-away gift of a box of note cards with wispy paintings of women on them. I didn't want to give her anything large that would stress her already bulging luggage. And I did hope that it would encourage her to write. I had thought about including a roll of postage stamps also, but money was a little tight that month, so I decided to leave it with just the box of cards. The women depicted on the cards were at ease in each other's company as they lounged and laughed and gazed off into the future together. I wanted them to remind Julia of our friendship. I didn't want to be left behind, like the plant.

At four o'clock I couldn't hold out any longer, I had to have something to eat. I pulled into the parking lot of the Madonna Inn, a god-awful pink establishment undoubtedly created by some lovesick husband trying to please his wife who was obviously partial to pink. It was favored by unimaginative honeymooners who couldn't wait to check into the safari room to play out their jungle kitten fantasies. I knew from my many trips between the Bay Area and L.A. that they had interesting bathrooms and a pretty decent salad bar. That would do for the time being. Being a veritable expert at salad bars, I was swift in my choices and was seated in record time. I took the opportunity to check my messages. There were no messages from Felicia, the rape counselor, or my office. There were two messages from Shelly, the latter sounding more urgent, so I called her. She answered on the second ring and launched right in.

"Paula, where is she?" she said in an unmistakably accusatory tone. I visualized her standing in the kitchen, one hand on her hip, foot tapping and chain smoking.

"It's not like I'm hiding her Shelly," I said, a bit too defensively. *Perhaps I was.*

"I get virtually nothing from her for two years, then this!" I knew she was waving the invitation at the telephone. I let the silence hang between us for a moment, so that she could compose herself.

"It's just that I really need her right now."

"Daryl?" I questioned, knowing good and well I needn't have asked.

"Yeah, of course Daryl, the bane of my existence. You don't know what I've been going through with him lately."

"I can imagine," I said pushing away my salad plate, I had either eaten too many garbanzo beans or the conversation had robbed me of my appetite, I wasn't sure which.

"I doubt it," she said, exhaling forcefully enough that I irrationally checked the receiver for escaping second-hand smoke.

"The man's insane, and I really need Julia's help with this . . . situation."

My concern right then was for Julia, and as far as I was concerned, Shelly would have to fend for herself awhile longer. "Shelly, Daryl is not Julia's responsibility. He's your husband and it's your life."

"Yes, but she's my sister!" *Sister, Mother, Savior, Scapegoat,* I silently filled in.

"I seem to remember that you were the one who decided to get back together with him in spite of all your sister's efforts to extract you from *the situation.*"

"Yes, well I thought . . . Oh, never mind. Will you ask her to call me please? I know that you must know where she is."

"I know that she won't be in the Bay Area for another two weeks."

She was silent for a moment, then said "I'm sorry Paula for putting this on you. I'm just frustrated. Then there's Mom on top of everything else."

*So she knew about Nora.* "How is Nora?" I asked, playing dumb.

"On her way out. Finally."

"What's the diagnosis?" *Dumb as a stick.*

"Breast cancer turned into lung cancer and now it's in her brain somewhere. If there's any justice in this world, she'll die because she can't get enough air. She'll just suffocate to death."

I was speechless. She went on. "The administrative staff of the hospital has been calling here, all concerned that neither of us has been around to see this *wonderful* dying woman. They say in all their years they've never seen anything like it. Finally I just told them flat out how it is."

"What did you say?"

"I told them that's what she gets for abusing her children their entire lives."

"I bet that shut them up."

"Damn straight."

In that Julia had, for all practical purposes, disappeared right after Turner's funeral, I'd had little opportunity to talk to her, console her in her grief, or basically to just check in with her from time to time to see how she was processing the whole experience. I had fully expected that I would be the one she would turn to, that I would be there while she healed. I was disappointed that I never had the opportunity, that I hadn't been there to feel that relief that one experiences as she realizes her best friend is turning the corner and is once again headed toward joy. As a friend, I felt I had been robbed of the experience. As a therapist, I was worried. No matter how you sliced it, in her hour of need she had struck out on her own, disassociating herself from the comfort found in the company of those who love her best.

I really didn't know what to expect, meeting her here in Malibu, two years after the fact, with nothing more than the casual postcard to fill in the blanks. When she first disappeared I had used up a sackful of emotions—concern had eventually turned to worry, and worry had a way of insidiously mounting to fear and panic when I was alone with my imaginings in the middle of the night. Whenever I'd get to the point of calling the American Embassies of The World to see if they knew anything of her whereabouts, I'd receive a rather generic fun-in-the-sun, wish-you-were-here type postcard with no return address.

The first few had arrived within a couple of months of each other. I read them over and over, searching for clues as to her state of mind. I analyzed her signature, comparing it to her former autograph to see if I could pick up any signs of distress, despondency or depression. I finally came to the conclusion after six months of scrutiny, that I knew nothing more about her feelings than I did the day she left. One Friday night, dateless and with a few glasses of wine under my belt, I sat on my sofa and began, in my frustration, to rip up her postcards. The first card I ever received, had been sent from Paris—I tore it into the smallest pieces I could manage. The second card was from Sitges and met a similar, although not so minute, fate. The third card, from Prague, I tucked into my purse and carried around with me for a week, before it finally came to rest permanently beneath a palm-tree magnet on my refrigerator door. I liked envisioning Julia living in a castle with turrets in the Staré Mésto.

I know about sorrow. I've been in practice long enough to see its many faces. I know it can be as concrete as Boulder Dam, as heavy as Cheops, and will mar the horizon of our lives like a parking lot at Macchu Picchu. And I know that the heaviness of it will eventually lift, but not before leaving in its place a bruised dent on the side of the heart that refuses to let go. No one is ever quite the same after the death of a spouse and Julia was no exception.

Their time together had been brief, just long enough to get in sync with each other. They were from different worlds, and after the first two years of precariously balancing misunderstandings and forgiveness, they learned to give themselves over to the wash of love that flowed around and through their marriage. It was as if the borders of their individual peculiarities had just begun to twine into a delicate grapevine weave, surrounding their union, giving it texture and stability. To put it another way, they had learned to take comfort in the fluid see-saw of relationship that only takes place when one fully trusts another's underlying motivation.

* * *

**We all had our doubts at first,** of course, when they married so abruptly. We were single, trying to sift through the fluff and bullshit to find the perfect mate. We had made lists and columns ranging from *what we absolutely required in a man* to *what we would not tolerate.* As the years came faster and faster, we began shifting the columns ever so slightly. It seemed our level of tolerance was improving on an annual basis. So when Julia, the quintessential California girl, came home married to a Texan, we couldn't help but roll our eyes.

We were expecting some love-at-first-sight missive. We should have known better. This is how she explained her marriage to a man she had just met and barely knew: "I believe in the elastic nature of time. Time is a continuum, stretched out before us like a line of rail headed straight for the heavens. And we, like so many railcars, move in and out of pre-existing scenarios based on where we find our selves on the track. All of life has already happened, and that 'future us' that has already experienced 'it' sometimes looks back and pokes her head into our present to alert us to future possibilities, giving us a wink and a gentle shove in a specific direction." The answer didn't quite satisfy. When questioned further, she simply replied, "I knew it was where I belonged."

I never tire of Julia's adventures, can hardly wait for the next installment. But when I visited her at her hilltop home in Penngrove soon after her marriage to Turner, I had to wonder at the set of circumstances that had turned my friend into a Miss Texas contestant, her hair and smile as stiff as ever seen this side of El Paso. I leaned forward in my chair to scrutinize this new Julia. Dressed in Paul Lauren bermuda shorts, a white Ashworth golf shirt and Ferragamo loafers, I hardly recognized her. Who was she kidding with those fiberglass overlays anyway? Certainly not me. She raised a glass of ice tea to her lips with an uncharacteristic crook to her little finger. She was Suddenly Southern. White washed verandas heavily hung with wisteria and Mint Juleps for everyone. I could almost smell magnolia blossoms and I was relatively certain that she had managed to obtain a slight drawl in the three months that she had been living with Turner in South Texas. Without warning or hesitation, my casual, *it is what it is* friend had become a poised and polished belle, a golfing belle it would seem.

Polished was never a word one would normally apply to Julia. Beautiful? Some would say so, in that casual California-girl sort of way. Maybe even stunning on a good day when she put some effort into it, which was rare. But POLISHED in that high society Old Money-Dallas way—never. There would always be the stray dog hairs on her black pants, and mustard would always make its way from her veggie-dog to her white blouse. As a matter of fact, I've never seen anyone lose the polish faster than Julia, regardless of the extent of her efforts to the contrary. She was the only woman I knew who could manage to scuff her high heel, break a nail, muss her hair and chew off her lipstick in the time it took her to glide down the staircase for her grand entrance. She never would have held up as a debutante. Cotillion balls were not for her. She was Grace Slick belting it out in Golden Gate Park, all flowered and beaded. In fact, she had always prided herself on being able to go from bed to door in under five minutes. Teeth brushed, comb through hair, lip gloss, jeans, sandals, T-shirt and Voila! If she could find her keys—five minutes; if not—well, then she was late.

* * *

**Just past the Grapevine** I dropped down into the valley and traffic slowed as commuters began to appear. I stopped at the Shell station to fill up and get something cold to drink. I couldn't resist a package of red whips, a sure sign that I was getting nervous. I hate that about myself. I'm Happy—Let's eat; I'm Sad—Better eat; I'm Nervous about seeing my best friend—Sounds like it's time for red whips to me! People say I'm too hard on myself, that I should ease up a little on my dietary restrictions and ease up a lot on my exercise mania. They might change their tune if they could see how I handle stress when no one is watching. Once I settled back into traffic, my thoughts returned to that day in Penngrove. That was, after all, the day I met Turner.

I studied her sipping her tea and absentmindedly twirling her new ring. The random twists and turns of Julia's life intrigued me. I suppose the reason her life looks different from most everyone else I know is because she unabashedly flings herself headlong and recklessly into situations which others might very well choose to avoid. She loves to challenge herself, always trusting that the cosmos will respond with some new insight. In her case the cosmos usually comes through. But now I was concerned that some terrible celestial snag had been hit. Of all the conceivable scenarios that I could have concocted, Julia married to a Texan was not one of them.

Raz, her faithful Rhodesian, sat at her feet, occasionally twitching and doggie talking in his sleep, locked in his private dream world of wild cat chases from his younger days. Buddy, a Rottweiler mix and five years his junior, still had the energy of a pup and made a great show of running and tossing his squeaky toy in the air, trying to engage us in a game of fetch. The newcomer and latest addition to Julia's four-legged family was Casey, Turner's dog, a four-pound prima donna of a Toy Pomeranian who, ignoring her new brothers, was snuggled down contentedly in Julia's lap.

"What's going on here?" I said through clenched teeth, hoping Turner wasn't eavesdropping.

"What do you mean?"

"Don't be obtuse. Why are you dressed like this? What's with the fluff ball on your lap? And look at your fingernails. Honestly Julia, how do you propose to work in the garden with those things?"

Shadow and light from the overhead pergola patterned her as she continued to play with her ring which caught a spark and momentarily flashed a golden beacon. A lighthouse in turbulent waters—five carat diamonds can do that. The full effect of the sun was inches from her face. She closed her eyes and positioned herself to take advantage of its warmth. I noticed a slight shimmer on her cheek.

"Don't tell me you're wearing face powder," I admonished, leaning in closer to exam her better. Eyes closed, she nodded. That's when I sighed, sat back, slumped.

"So what was it in that one moment when you first met him that made you run to the MAC counter at Macy's?"

"Paula."

"Let me re-phrase. How did you know he was The One?"

"I just knew," she said, stroking Casey's head.

"Not good enough. Try again," I said. I knew her better than to think it had anything to do with his money. Money had never impressed her much. She had walked away from suitors other women would have considered lottery jackpots. Sure, like most

Homo sapiens she enjoyed money and the freedom that came with it, but she had always had a take-it-or-leave-it attitude.

The thing that stands out in my memory about that day was the inconsistency of it all. That, and the fact that I never really got an answer that satisfied. Until then, nothing she had ever done surprised me or those who knew her. If she got what she considered a good idea, she acted upon it immediately. By the time the thought hit the floor she was already out the door. We wouldn't have been at all surprised, given her tendencies and beliefs, to someday learn that she had become a monkess, walking away from all her worldly possessions, preferring to live alone in the side of a cliff, wearing white robes and performing sun salutations each morning. Needless to say, face powder and fiberglass nails were incompatible with that image.

The way I recall it, the reason I never got a satisfactory answer is because we were interrupted when Turner walked out onto the deck. Turner: tall, handsome, sure. His blue jeans were freshly and crisply starched from the dry cleaners. This was a new one on me. I had never seen nor heard of such a thing. Californians try to keep their clothes as soft and relaxed as they strive to be. The term "stiff" is reserved for upper lips, alcoholic beverages, and the preferred state of male genitalia—never jeans.

"Hey Darlin'," he said, white teeth gleaming, "You two ladies havin' yourselves a little hen party out here?"

I could tell he thought the two of us were cute as buttons and figured that any discussion two *ladies* might be having, would necessarily be frivolous and amusing. I resisted the urge to tell him the hens were busy debating the relativity theory as applies to black holes, choosing instead to smile back up at him, sweetly, just like Julia.

It took longer than I remembered to get through the greater L.A. area on a Friday evening. The traffic was making me crazy and before I completely gave myself over to road rage I decided to throttle back a notch or two with a little soothing music. I wasn't expected in Malibu until later that evening, I reminded myself, and made a concerted effort to relax as I inched my way down Hwy 405 to the Santa Monica Freeway. I could tell from our recent phone conversation that Julia was ready to talk about her relationship with Turner, so by the time I reached the Pacific Coast Highway I had mentally reviewed what little I knew of her scant three years with him.

Julia, an inveterate traveler, is never happier than when she has a daypack on her back, a camera in her hand and an unexplored road ahead of her. Her goal has always been to see as much of the planet as possible in the time allotted her this life. She has the most extensive collection of travel brochures of anyone I've ever known. She never missed the Sunday edition travel section of the San Francisco Examiner, leaving the balance of the paper unread kindling. When she was in town, I knew I could find her Sunday mornings sprawled out on her living room floor clipping and filing. Not unlike those who clip coupons, she clipped destinations, organizing and safeguarding them as if they were foreign currency.

Fortunately she figured out how to support herself and her habit simultaneously. After college she hired on as a photographer for "Gaia," an off-shoot of "National Geographic" dedicated to lifestyles of women around the globe. She and her camera explored the day-to-day life of women from Papua New Guinea to Quintana Roo. She'd return from a trip bursting with enthusiasm over some new skill she had learned. Once she even tried flooding her backyard in an attempt to grow her own rice, an endeavor that quickly proved to be more trouble than it was worth. She was happy at "Gaia" and they were thrilled to have her on board, her eye for the abstract and her mastery of lighting made her a favorite of the travel writers associated with the magazine.

The only glitch in the life that she created for herself was the weather. The fact that it got cold certain times of the year annoyed her. She became uncomfortable and irritable whenever the temperature dipped below fifty degrees, and she never got the hang of dressing properly to ward it off. She is a shorts and sandals girl—always will be. Her idea of bundling up is to wear a bra. Frosty locales were just not in her future.

After turning down more than a couple of cold weather assignments, she came to realize that if she was going to be so picky she'd need to start supplementing her income. It was for this very reason she began branching into other areas of photography. About the time she turned forty, she was firmly established as a *name* in fine art photography. She created abstract visions that would take the viewer to the magical recesses of her mind. In her wall-size photo collages, symbols mixed with landscapes superimposed over women's bodies. It was hard to separate nature from the image of woman in her work. Her goal had been to empower women by illustrating their link to nature—the part of woman that remains eternal and true, regardless of what has been taken from her.

She was hugely successful. It wasn't long before she earned enough to buy herself a lovely home in the hills of Sonoma County. She traveled whenever she pleased, and always during the winter months when Northern California temperatures forced her to warmer climates. Mexico had always captivated her, and once she found the seaside area around Manzanillo with its Moorish architecture and cobblestone streets, she claimed it as her winter hideout and leased a small condo on the beach every winter until it warmed up enough to go home—or wherever else she fancied.

It was there, in the winter of 1996 that she met Turner. He was overnighting at Las Hadas resort, at the tale end of a business trip, when his business associates talked him into attending the Thursday night fashion show. The event was held outdoors in the Doña Albina courtyard. Julia knew the local designers and bartered her photographic services for some flashy Mexican dresses she would never wear anywhere but in Mexico. The minute he laid eyes on her he began a hard sell and full press to make her his wife. The day after he returned home to the border town of McAllen, the DHL packages began arriving daily at Julia's condo. He overwhelmed her with a profusion of love letters and recorded love songs played on his guitar. He sent photos, sensitive cards and little heart-shaped ruby earrings. He had a local florist flood her condo with exotic flowers. After all, he was a business man. He knew how to close a deal. He returned to Manzanillo every Thursday and stayed until the following Monday morning. After three weeks of this he popped the question. She accepted on the spot and they were married at the McAllen Country Club a few weeks later.

If he had known her as well as I know her, he wouldn't have gone to so much trouble. For on that very day, the day of their first meeting, Julia had spent an interesting hour with La Señora, wherein she learned in no uncertain terms that she would meet the love of her life *muy pronto*, if not that very evening. She was told to pay particular attention to the man's wrist which would bear symbols—of what, La Señora was not sure. Julia erroneously interpreted this piece of information to mean that her new love would be a Jewish concentration camp survivor, his number tattooed on his wrist. She was less than zealous about the prospect. She had visited Anne Frank's home in Amsterdam and she had seen "Sophie's Choice." And although she was sympathetic to what those poor people had endured, she was hoping, given her own disastrous beginnings, to link arms with someone from a more traditional past.

Still, she had learned in the years that followed her time with Nora, to trust life and the subtle directives offered from on high. So it was with an expectancy, if not enthusiasm, that she made herself up and went out that evening in search of her new Jewish husband. When Turner appeared at her side—tall, handsome and Waspish—Julia was prepared to dismiss him less she end up in an entanglement that would keep her from her destiny. But he was persistent and after the show when she had a minute to sit down and relax, he arrived once again at her side, this time with a glass of Chardonnay. She thanked him, and as she reached for the glass he offered, she noticed his shirt sleeve. The cuff bore his monogram in a swirl of symbols at his wrist. Couple that with a smile that stopped her heart, and the forthcoming DHL packages were truly superfluous.

To the best of my knowledge the two of them were successful in merging their wildly divergent lifestyles into a harmonious union. She would have preferred that they leave South Texas to the armadillos and make Northern California their home, but Turner's roots were deep and clustered with friends and family, not to mention his railcar leasing business which, although he could oversee from afar, he preferred to administrate in person. They struck a compromise that had them bouncing back and forth randomly, the upshot being that I had a difficult time keeping track of her whereabouts.

After witnessing her Miss Texas impersonation, I just had to visit her there to see for myself what her new life looked like. She picked me up in her Jeep one muggy December morning at the Harlingen Airport. As we drove through fields of sorghum and aloe vera, past longhorns and egrets and long canals called resacas, I had an opportunity to size her up without being too obvious. Although she was still sporting those nails, I was happy to see that her hair was not as stiff. It was, however, bigger than I'd ever seen her wear it before.

Thankfully her makeup had toned down and I could see more of the old Julia showing through. We passed more than one "Don't Mess With Texas" bumper sticker, a trailer park called the "Holiday Out," *ha ha*, and numerous tire repair shops along the side of the road, one of which was owned by three guys named Gooley, Dickey and Tickey. I was getting thirsty driving by all the parched landscape and was having a hard time imagining Julia living in a place that failed to soothe her with greenery. We stopped at Karla's Kuntry Kitchen to get something to drink. The woman behind the counter wore her glory days proudly on her ample chest.

Right next to her name tag, "Verna Jean," was a pin that claimed her as an "Ex-Dallas Cowboy Cheerleader." I was soon to learn that all the girls in Texas had two names and used them both, like Tami Jo, and Lucy May. Even the streets had middle names: Georgia Ruth, Carla Lorraine and Vicki Lynn.

"What can I getcha, Darlin'?" she asked me as I stared at her bright blue eyeshadow. I couldn't help but think that she'd be pretty if she'd just tone down the makeup and spend a few hours a week on the stairmaster.

"I'll have a coke to go, please." She wrote it down.

"What kind?" she asked.

"Excuse me?" Up until then I had thought that a coke was a coke was a coke. Julia intervened. "I'll have a Dr. Pepper and she'll have a Coca-Cola." She smiled at my confusion. "Coke is a generic term down here for any soft drink that's not a Dr. Pepper," she explained. While we waited on Verna Jean, I surveyed the counter which was laden with various flyers. In my perusal I learned that I had just missed the Cockroach Festival that had been held at the McAllen Civic Center the week before and that it was not too late to sign up for Snake Training Classes.

"What do they train snakes to do?" I asked, my interest seriously aroused.

"Silly, you can't train a snake. But you can train people to deal with snake bites and educate them as to how to avoid bites in the first place." She pointed to her rather impenetrable looking boots, "see, snake boots." I marveled at her substantial footwear. My own feet in their new two-tone Joan and David's suddenly looked particularly vulnerable.

"Don't worry, Sissy. We'll getcha all fixed up." She slung her arm around my shoulders and steered me toward the door, while I stared at the ground, expecting a snake attack with every step.

"Say hey to Tres for me," Verna Jean called out to us, as she leaned over the counter, showing more cleavage than was generally acceptable at eleven o'clock in the morning.

Julia waved back at her and said in a good ol' gal kinda way, "Well, ain't you the rhymin' fool, Verna Jean?" Verna Jean chuckled and waved us goodbye.

"Say hey to whom?" I asked, as we pulled back onto the long, straight, flat Texas highway.

"Tres," she said, pronouncing it like the plastic rectangles people use to set their plate on in a cafeteria line. "It never ceases to amaze me how many people whom I've never met know I'm married to Turner."

"Uh huh, but who's Tres?"

"That's Turner. That's what they call him round these parts," she said with an affected drawl.

"Why?"

"It's short for Turner David Parks, III. Everybody calls him Tres, but me."

"And you don't because . . . ?"

"It feels diminutive to me. It's like reducing a person as powerful as Turner to a number, like someone with a white paper tag waiting for a sandwich at a deli counter. The South seems to favor this unimaginative naming of the first boy, third generation in a family of . . . oh, say, Billy Bobs, for example." I laughed, which proved she was achieving her goal, so she continued.

"Yes, let's see, first comes Billy Bob, Sr., followed by Billy Bob II; then presumably for convenience sake, instead of Billy Bob III, the poor child is dubbed Tres—number three—just Tres." She continued in her best documentary voice, "In the South there are many of these numbered children: Tres Williams, Tres Jones, Tres Whatever. So in a nation where every boy and every team wants to be Number One . . ." she held up her right index finger, "the Tres' of the world are reminded subtly and daily that in some very fundamental way they will never be Numero Uno."

I wondered if the name Tres reminded her that he is her third husband. Probably not.

"The name Tres has become so common, due largely to the male ego wishing to reproduce itself over and over again, that there are derivatives of the derivative. While the Northerners will have their Maxwell Parker Abernathy the III's—they're proud of their roman numerals in the North, you see—the South, on the other hand has C.E.O.'s named anything from Trey to Trace. Not even a whole Billy Bob, just a hint, a ghost, a mere smudge of one. A Trace."

"Well, from what little I've seen of Turner, he doesn't appear to be lacking in the self confidence department."

"No, you're right. He absolutely is not."

I thought she proclaimed the latter a little forcefully, and wondered what was behind it. "That Verna Jean ever date Turner, you think?"

"How would I know? It's a small place. I'm sure he dated a lot of women. He's the kiss and don't tell kinda fellow."

"How would you know?! If it were me I'd know every last one's name, date of birth, how many times they had sex, what positions, and last but not least, I'd want to know the present whereabouts of any old flames within a ten-mile radius. I wouldn't want any surprises. I wouldn't want to spend an evening talking to some nice woman at the Cattle Baron's Ball, only to find out later that she was the love of his life. Aren't you even curious?"

"About Verna Jean? Really Paula."

"About Verna Jean, yes, about Verna Jean and her double D's. She is about the right age, and was probably a looker in her cheerleading days."

"I'm not worried."

"I don't mean you should be worried, Julia," I said with a heavy sigh, "I just think if I were in your shoes I'd be collecting data."

"For what purpose? I know where I stand with Turner. And the way I look at it, any woman he was with before me taught him a little something about women and hopefully a little about himself. If it weren't for those other women he wouldn't be the man he is today."

"Well, I wish I had your casual attitude, but I'm not wired that way."

"It's just that you chose to see other women as competition. My advice to you is to chose again, Paula."

"I guess you're right."

"Of course I'm right. I've known you for a good many years, my friend, and I've seen how your jealousies have worked against you."

We drove in silence for all of sixty seconds with the KTEX radio station for background filler. A rousing tune about a girl thinking a guy's tractor is sexy sent us both into fits of laughter. "Hey, do you have any Bubba's down here?" I asked.

"Yep. We've go us one Big Daddy Lawton, too."

"No kiddin'?"

"That's no joke, Sissy."

They lived in a condo on South Padre Island, but to say so doesn't do their accommodations justice. A more accurate mental picture is formed when you add that the condo is over four thousand square feet. The condo itself sits three stories high, each floor with a balcony overlooking the bay. The floors are connected by a private elevator or spiral staircase, take your pick. Aside from the area Julia had appropriated for her darkroom, Turner used the lower level for his office. The deck at that level extends out into the bay forming a private dock for, what else, his yacht. During the tour I noticed one suite of rooms that was decorated with plastic flowers and a weeping Jesus. Atypical Julia decor, so I asked her about it.

"These are Maria's rooms." Should have known. Maria was the live-in maid. I immediately stopped worrying about Julia roughing it in sagebrush country. Maria took good care of me the week I was there. It was sort of like living in a hotel; the bed was turned down every night, no mints, but-oh-well. My clothes were unpacked and re-pressed by the time I finished my first Lone Star beer. I began fantasizing about turning my junk room back home into a maid's quarters, then I came to my senses. Not only am I not of the temperament to have someone underfoot, the cost of such a service in California would set me back more than I'd even care to think about.

"I think I'll go for a run on the beach," I announced the first morning after my arrival.

"*Pero*, it's 9 a.m.," Maria flatly stated—a seeming non-sequitur—in the typical Tex-Mex mixture of English and Spanish prevalent along the Rio Grande. I returned an hour later, drenched and panting, ready to pass out from the humidity and heat.

"Hey there darlin'," Julia said, wearing her fake Texas accent. She knew I secretly feared she'd just one day turn into a Texan and that would be the last any of us would see of her. "Better go earlier next time," she said, watching me pant and handing me a glass of water.

"Check."

"That heat's a surprise, isn't it Paula?" Turner said as he poured himself another cup of coffee with chicory. "Fooled Julia more than once, didn't it Hon?"

"Yep."

"Remember your first dinner party?" he asked, chuckling to himself.

"Fraid so," she replied.

"What happened?" I asked, helping myself to another glass of water.

"A fiasco," she said, lips pursed to one side.

"She made sushi," Turner filled in. "Spent all day getting it just right."

"I love your sushi," I said, wistfully remembering the first time she had made it for me. The compact, perfect tubes she rolled still shine in my memory, especially compared to the misshapen, rice-falling-out-everywhere version I seem to always produce.

"I forgot my audience," she said, hoping I'd catch on. When I didn't, she leaned over the counter and yelled "Raw fee-ish!! I thought one woman was going to puke all over her cashmere sweater. All those beautiful little makis down the disposal."

"And she served it outdoors!" he laughed, like it was something strange, as if the concept was too barbaric to even contemplate within the confines of polite society.

"So?" I said, coming to her defense. "What's the problem with that?"

"The problem is that it was July," he said, as if that explained everything.

I looked over at Julia, who simply said, "Heat, humidity, an assortment of insects, most of which are in search of blood. And," she went on, "as no one eats outdoors in the summer, the women weren't prepared. They expected to be indoors where it's always freezing." I noted that I was standing with my arms folded across my chest to ward off the artificial chill from the air conditioning which blasted every home and business establishment, every day of every year. "One woman had actually worn a long-sleeved merino with a high racoon collar."

"Hmm, I see."

"That was mink, darlin'," Turner chimed in.

"It was my first summer. I thought everyone would appreciate the sunset."

"The guys on the golf course are still talking about the raw fish," Turner said, shaking his head. *Ah Lucy, my simple little wife*, he might have said.

I was starting to feel a bit queasy myself.

"Now I just let Turner grill'em up some T-bones and everyone's happy. They're partial to beef and diamonds down here, you know," she said, waving her left hand at nothing in particular. Her ring, as if on cue, and to add emphasis to the point, caught a glimmer of light and fractured it into a rainbow spectrum of tiny bright flecks which momentarily transited the wall by which she stood.

"My, my, my," was all I could think to say.

By the end of my week's visit I had witnessed my fill of big blonde hair, big hats, big belt buckles, big mosquitos. Having lived in L. A. I was use to big boobs. I had learned to eat tamales which arrived by the dozens at Julia's door, handmade and hand delivered by a local Mexican woman. Maria apparently drew the line when it came to certain chores, and tamales, an art form in Texas, was something she just wasn't willing to make. Somehow Julia had managed to talk the old woman into making a batch of vegetarian tamales just for me. The woman looked at me sideways. Evidently if you didn't eat beef you were automatically pegged as being not Texan, something forgivable but not entirely beyond suspicion.

I could see that Julia seemed to be adjusting to her new life. As a child she had learned to be a chameleon from all the bouncing around and changing of residences. Couple that with her innate confidence in the divine order of things and it wasn't as hard on her as it would have been for someone else, like me, for example.

When it was time to go, I was ready. By then I had been "Mam'd" to the point of distraction. "That'll be $19.53, Mam." "Would you like paper or plastic, Mam?" "Did you find everything all right, Mam?" "Just sign here, Mam." "Would you like help out with that, Mam?"

"Stop Mamming me," I hissed at a startled box boy at the local H.E.B supermarket. I couldn't quite get use to the way they spoke. It didn't seem to offend her that I considered, albeit unfairly, their speech patterns lazy and uneducated. She found their manner of expression charming and natural. "You just have to relax, no stiff enunciations, lips parted only slightly, and let the words slip out across your tongue. They'll just naturally come out Southern," she explained. She had obviously practiced a good deal, although she wasn't fooling anyone into thinking she was a local.

I did walk away with one useful turn of phrase, I have to admit. That multi-purpose pronoun, "Y'all," had managed to creep into my vernacular. I found it useful in that it covers all pertinent parties in one fell swoop. "Where y'all goin' this summer?" was a time saver when compared to "Where are you and John and the kids and the grandparents going this summer." Made sense to me. This tickled Julia no end. At the airport she teased me by presenting me with a T-shirt that read "I wasn't born in Texas, but I got here as soon as I could."

I still have the T-shirt, had even thought about bringing it to Malibu for a laugh, but in the end I left it behind. That was my one and only trip to Texas, but it served its purpose. I had to see for myself how she was pulling off the Southern Wife thing. I didn't want to see her slip away in the process. I needed to know that everything I had learned from her over the years was real.

It was eight o'clock before I pulled up in front of the Malibu Beach Inn. The innkeeper insisted that Julia Parks had not checked in. I gave her my last name and told her we had reserved a suite. Upon checking further she handed me a room key and told me that a Ms. Julia La Chance had indeed arrived earlier that day. She had returned to her maiden name, the one she had cleverly abandoned in grade school.

I found our suite easily enough, it being one of two on the top floor of the tiny hotel. I pushed open the door, expectantly calling her name. No response. The remains of a fire gave a soft welcoming glow to the living room. A note taped to the bathroom mirror welcomed me and informed me that she was walking the beach and would be back soon. From the sound of the surf crashing I knew that she had left the doors to our balcony wide open. I stepped outside and let the saltwater breeze wash through me, clearing my head of traffic jams, Felicia and other concerns. *I'm going to see Julia.* I looked up and down the beach, which was already dark this time of year, hoping to find her returning from her walk.

As she was nowhere to be seen, I quickly unpacked, noting that she had left the preferred bed, the one closest to the balcony, for me.

On my pillow she had placed a white hibiscus. I'm always a bit surprised whenever people take the time to be that thoughtful and considerate. I wonder at myself for not being the type of person that thinks ahead to do those little things that make another feel special and loved. Even worse, sometimes I actually think of some sweet gesture, but don't feel sufficiently motivated to carry it through. But that was another of Julia's talents; she made everyone feel special.

While using the bathroom, I took a quick inventory of her toiletries. Nothing too exotic, the basics really. Cosmetics added up to a scant showing of lip gloss, a worn down to the nub eyeliner and Mac blush, color: prism. No hydroxy anything. My toiletry bag looked like a suitcase next to hers. I started lining up all my beauty products on my side of the sink, then stopped. Feeling silly and a little embarrassed by the sheer number of bottles and tubes, I put some back in my suitcase. I'm a sucker for all sorts of beauty aids, especially those little bags of freebies that come *with your purchase of $18 or more.* I can't seem to rid myself of the thought that the adolescent working the beauty counter at Nieman's is holding out on me, hiding some magic cream under the counter on purpose. I'm not really a paranoid individual, but I want to believe that there's some product out there somewhere that will truly minimize these character lines that life keeps laying down. And I can't get over the idea that the beauty counter girl knows, but just won't tell. Probably stockpiling for herself and her friends. The end result is that I overspend. Julia, obviously, had not fallen prey to that trap, at least not since her Texas days.

I grabbed my jacket and headed down to the large surfside veranda off the lobby. I ordered a cup of hot tea and found a seat under one of those metallic mushrooms that somehow manages to heat even the coolest nights. I studied my nails and feigned interest in the overweight pug that was suppose to be lying obediently at the feet of his master, but kept sniffing my shoes instead. All this to keep from craning my neck down the beach in anticipation of her arrival. I sipped my tea, added more Sweet-N-Low, fidgeted, glared at a hangnail. I thought of Nora and how startled I had been to run into her at the hospital. I wondered for the umpteenth time whether or not I should tell Julia about the encounter, or just let it wait until Shelly came at her with the news. I was relatively certain Julia had no way of knowing about her mother's condition, having cut off all contact many years before. Thinking of Nora was not one of my favorite pastimes in that it inevitably led to my thinking of the abuse Julia sustained as a child. As far as I'm concerned, whatever pain Nora's in, she deserves.

Finally, before I had an opportunity to get myself too worked up over Nora's despicable treatment of her two daughters, I spotted Julia making her way toward the veranda. She hadn't yet seen me when I jumped up, spilling tea down the front of my white pants. *Big deal, so what. Was this fastidious me talking?* I just couldn't sit there cooly distracted, waiting for her to brush the sand off her bare feet and discover me casually waiting, so blasé.

I could tell, even from a distance, that she had aged five years in the two she had been gone. She had a wanderer's look about her:

weathered skin, a little gaunt in the face, hair straggling down her back. In her faded Levi's jacket and rolled-up drawstring pants she resembled a peace corps worker returned from the field and altogether unprepared for the metropolitan hustle and pace.

I ran to her, mentally speed dialing The Salon to set up her future appointments. Her sobs began the moment I reached her, held her close and took in the heady, exotic scent of her. The powerful, self-assured woman I had always admired seemed delicate and fragile. As we unashamedly wept and held each other, I forgot about the pug nibbling my sandal and Julie's need for beauty services, my only concern to protect her and keep her from anyone or anything that might cause her more pain.

We were up late that evening trying to catch up with the events of our respective lives over the last two years. My life had been rather uneventful, especially compared to Julia's, just one failed romance after the other, nothing new to report really. Still, she listened with interest and when it was her turn she filled me in on her time in Paris, the hours and days that she had roamed the streets with her camera, trying to find her place there amongst her imagined ancestors. She tried to make sense of Turner's death and their marriage cut short. She had cursed the heavens for robbing her of the comfortable golden years she had envisioned sharing with him. This didn't sound like the Julia I know. When I asked her gently what happened to *it is what it is*, she replied that sometimes the torch is just too heavy and you have to lay it down. Restless and unfulfilled she had wandered through Europe for the better part of a year, before finally making her way back to Manzanillo, where she had tried in vain to return to the carefree lifestyle she had lived before Turner's death. There was a shadow that followed her now, she explained, something that she couldn't quite shake.

"It's as though my past has finally reached out far enough to claim me," she told me over breakfast the next morning. "I have moments of joy, but I can't seem to sustain them."

Turner's death had definitely thrown her for a loop. To make matters more complicated, some psychic had told her she was sure to re-marry by the end of the year. Never mind that she wasn't seeing anyone, Julia was still trusting enough to believe that sometime within the next eight weeks she was going to meet a guy, fall in love and marry him before the year was over. My assignment, as she saw it, was to help her put her house in order, clear the decks and make ready for the next phase she saw herself entering. I assured her I was up to the challenge, although she seemed a bit off and I wasn't exactly certain what I was getting myself into.

* * *

**That next evening,** we sat at dusk on a broad golden strip of California coastline. She sifted sand through her long fingers. I was glad to see the fiberglass overlays were history. They looked great on me, but on her they had always seemed inappropriate.

Beneath her jean jacket, Julia wore a faded blue work shirt over a pair of white, loose-fitting beachcombers. Her hair had always been an interesting mixture of gold tones, but age had darkened it to something resembling woodgrain with the reddish highlights of her youth now peaking through as silvery splinters of light. Her eyes, still as clear and arresting as when I first met her back in college, reflected the fading hues of the day. Her tan face reminded me of mid-summer instead of early November. I had already duly chastised her for her lack of skin care earlier that day, as all girlfriends are supposed to do for one another, and she had sworn that she'd started using sun screen a year ago. "Not soon enough," I had said, pointing out the hyperpigmentation on her face. "Oh," she replied, staring into our bathroom mirror. "Hmm, I thought I just had a new batch of freckles."

"Tell me about your father," I said. Her name change had been niggling me, especially since it dawned on me that I knew nothing about her father. I repositioned my feet so they sat neatly atop the beach, assuring myself that my persimmon-colored toe polish was indeed dry enough not to be ruined by the coarse sand. Julia ladeled handfuls of beach over her feet, which I noticed were calloused and from the tan lines looked like she had spent the last two years in flipflops. I watched, from the corner of my eye, for her initial response to my question.

She smiled and the lines around her eyes deepened, bird wings taking to the sky, "Not all that much to tell. Haven't I mentioned him before?"

"Somehow we managed to skip that page."

"I've always loved my father," she began. "He's been my blonde Adonis, my darling and handsome athlete, my prize winner and my strength." I nodded and shifted to face her, eager to hear more about this great guy, thankful for a story from her life that would make her smile. "Above all else, he held my hope. He was the one that got away."

"Got away?" I asked somewhat puzzled, my Freudian training kicking in. I resisted the urge to whip out a pad and start jotting down notes.

"Got away from my Mom and the life I was forced to live in her house."

"You mean he abandoned you?" I said, irritated that the story had already taken a turn for the worse.

"That's not how I see it. Let's move." She rose, not bothering to brush the sand from her butt. I followed, shaking, stomping and brushing at my pants, glad to be moving on to what I considered a more comfortable setting like our hotel veranda, and a glass of Chardonnay. Julia walked ten feet closer to the water and plopped herself down in sand that was decidedly damp. I looked longingly up the beach to the hotel and the outdoor firepit that was bathing the veranda in a warm glow. My longing went unnoticed, and as a testament to our friendship and just to underline what a super therapist I am, I kept it to myself, took a deep breath and plunked down next to her. The dampness immediately claimed both cheeks. She obviously had wanted sand that was a bit more malleable to assist her in telling her story, and as I'd taken a weekend seminar in Sand Tray Therapy I was intrigued by the shapes that began to take form. *Too bad there aren't little plastic Dad figures I could give her to act upon the stage she was creating.*

"I'm my father's daughter," she stated softly but clearly.

"Good," I said, encouragingly.

"I have his cheekbones. His eyes were a different color than mine—more a light blue, crystalline, but similar in shape." She used the past tense, so I mentally jotted a note, *deceased?* "He was a good man," she said, looking past me down the beach. I had the urge to look in the same direction to find him striding toward us. "Proud, somewhat arrogant," she said wistfully. "The stories my mother told wouldn't lead the ordinary listener to believe in his goodness. But I was able to read between the lines—his reasons for going—and I found a parent worth loving there. Like I said, he was my strength." She was making channels and miniature walls in the sand, shaping and molding them to her liking.

"How old were you when he left?" I asked, trying to discern what the walls were holding in, or keeping at bay.

"I was about six months old," came the reply. I was shocked. I had imagined a relationship.

"Did he visit often?" I asked hopefully.

"No, only once actually." Another wall went up. "Once when I was five. But he did try to kidnap me when I was a baby. I like that story a lot. Not that there's much of a story, it's his trying that matters. Of course my mother wouldn't let him take me—not her baby girl. She didn't realize at the time that she didn't like kids." A wall had begun to enclose the smaller walls, making a compound of sorts, or perhaps a maze.

"I remember every detail of that visit. I knew he was coming to see me and I made a big to-do over my appearance that day. I combed and re-combed my hair trying to make it lay down flat, not curl. I had on a blue and white flowered dress, white socks with little blue flowers around the cuff and black patent-leather shoes with straps. I was busy playing with my tea set when he arrived. Madlyn, the babysitter, let him in. I became aware of his presence like a shock. I turned to look up at a face that I would always remember. He was tall and tan. His blonde hair was streaked with so many different shades of gold I wanted to touch it to see if it was real. But the best part was that he was holding a dark green leather rocking chair just my size. I remember feeling shy and staring at my shoes. I hoped that he would like me, that I would somehow be engaging enough that he would want to stay with me."

We sat in silence while she composed herself. Finally she cleared her throat and continued. "In those days my mom was prone to wake me up at night to watch old movies with her. I didn't mind, it made me feel like I was her pal. I guess I had just seen one too many Shirley Temple movies." I laid my hand over hers.

"He just stood there staring at me. Then he knelt down, touched my calf and raised my foot a few inches off the ground. I grabbed hold of the back of my new chair to steady myself, and then I heard him say it, those words that I knew meant I had lost him for good. He said 'Your legs are like your mother's.' I pulled my leg away, but the examination continued. He brushed my bangs away from my forehead, looked straight into my eyes and said 'Your forehead is hers too.' I said nothing, feeling if the examination continued I would burst into tears. He really had nothing to say to me. How could he explain to his five-year-old daughter his reasons for leaving? How could he justify his absence? How could he speak of love to a little person he didn't know, one who was turning out so much like the woman he had escaped. I didn't know what to do or say. I continued to stare at the blue flowers on my socks, and eventually he leaned down, kissed my cheek, and left."

"My mother found me crying in front of the mirror later that evening. I was frantically combing my bangs in an attempt to cover my forehead and busy hating my thin little legs. She tried to console me by telling me not to cry that my father didn't love me and wasn't worth crying over. 'After all, he's never spent a penny on your support!' Which, of course, did nothing to ease my sense of rejection. After that she would spend years trying to keep the hair off my forehead and out of my eyes." She turned to me, fluffing her long bangs, a triumphant smile on her face, "As you can see, it didn't work."

I was shocked that she had chosen to identify with and love a parent with whom she'd had such little contact, and one that had, from a child's point of view, rejected her to boot. Then again, I was perplexed by the fact that this was the first I had heard of her father and her feelings for him.

"What are you making there?" I asked, pointing to the channels she had created in sand while she told her story.

"It's a house, see?" She pointed out the rooms, one by one. An architect's sandy mock-up. In the perfect house wouldn't you say that everything would flow," she waved her hand through the maze, "kitchen to dining room to living room, flowing into and out of atriums, right here, and into master suites and darkroom . . ."

"Dark room?" I imagined Julia huddled in a corner. Then I remembered.

"Well, in my perfect house anyway. Paula, home is a place I keep trying to find. I keep looking and searching. I am endlessly pawing through real estate guides trying to imagine how my life would look if I lived in that flowered Victorian, that Marin Tudor, or that hut on Phi Phi Island."

"Or imagining yourself warm and cozy in front of a roaring fire, perhaps," I said gesturing to the hotel, "instead of sitting here in the damp and cold."

"Oh, OK. Sorry. Let's head back." She put her arm around me trying to keep me warm as we strolled back. We passed by the veranda just long enough to snag a couple glasses of Rombaurer Chardonnay and some pretzels, before heading up to our room with its fireplace and solitude.

Once we'd changed into something less soggy, we raided the mini bar of its chocolate, lit the fire, and picked up where we left off.

"Paula, I have a confession."

"Yes?" I said encouragingly, the therapist in me hoping for a fissure in the rockface where I could easily sink my piton.

"I apartment shop in my dreams." I tried not to laugh, I'd heard many confessions, but seldom any as benign as this. "I decorate new rooms while I sleep. I figure out the finances of how to afford the place on dream calculators."

"Finances? But Julia, surely you're not hurting for money. You can live anywhere you choose."

"I know, I know. I keep feeling like if I can find this magical place, I'll finally feel safe. I'll belong. I'll fit. Hand-in-glove, lock-in-key kind of fit. I just can't seem to get there," she said, looking unsettled suddenly, restless.

"OK, two questions. First, why apartment? And second, what are the finances like?"

"I know this will sound strange, after all, Turner left me well cared for."

"Don't forget you made your mark and were doing fine before Turner."

"That's true. God I miss him."

"What do you miss most?"

"The security. I felt safe with him. Three years! That's all I got!" She shook her head as if safety was something that would always elude her. "Paula, when I shop in my dreams, I use the budget I had when I left my mother's house and was first on my own and all I could afford was a studio apartment."

"I keep searching for this place that eludes me, this feeling of belonging, this feeling of being home at last and at peace. I'm beginning to think it's not a place I'm going to find in the earth plane, I'm starting to think I'll only find it on the other side."

"What are you saying?" I asked. "Other side? Julia, you scare me when you talk this way," I said, remembering her suicide attempt, and feeling a chill run the length of my spine. That was nearly thirty years ago and she had since moved past my brother like a whirlwind. She never looked back, assuring me that was one chapter of her life that was closed for good. I wasn't so sure.

"Don't look so concerned, I'm not a twenty-year-old lame-brained romantic anymore. I know better than to go there again." She half-chuckled to herself, and stared into the fire. I waited for more, still as a stone. Sometimes the best thing I can do as a therapist is sit in silence while my client finds the words to express her inner turmoil.

"I guess I'm just weary. Tired of pushing down old feelings for which I have no use. That's why I called you, Paula. I've distracted myself for the last two years and after everything I've done and seen, when I look in the mirror I still see the same anguished face I saw the day of Turner's death. I sense that I'm sitting at a crossroad. I need to either get on with the business of living or . . ." She shook her head.

"Or what?"

"I don't know. Sit and watch the clock tick off the hours of my life, I guess. It's just that sometimes I feel like I've already lived the life I signed on for, and now I'm playing this waiting game, until my time's up."

In all the years I'd known her, I had never seen her so apathetic. The it-is-what it-is girl was nowhere in sight. "This doesn't sound like you," I offered.

"You're right, it's not my idea of me either, that's why I'm a little scared. It seems that when I wasn't looking, my childhood tapped me on the shoulder, whispering, 'Gotcha'." She swirled the wine in her glass. "Damn it, Paula, I'm fifty-two years old and I'm apartment shopping in my dreams. I feel like I've been living a life that's less than honest. I've been reluctant, hell, terrified, to think about my past. But my time's up, I've got to figure out who I am before I can go forward. Certainly before I can get married again."

I got the picture. And I knew we had a lot of work ahead of us. But I also know that timing is critical, and this particular evening would be best spent getting our rhythm down, getting in step with one another again. More to the point, perhaps, is that by the time she clued me in to her state of mind, we had already finished our wine and popped the cork on a bottle of Korbel. Personal ethics prevent me from conducting sessions while intoxicated, so I put away my mental notebook. Tonight we would play.

We had just polished off a large bag of M&M's and were about to round out our minimum daily requirements with a little protein from a bag of Cheetos when we heard a rather intense knocking at the door of our suite. We jumped and I guiltily hid the Cheetos behind my back, fantasizing that my personal trainer had gotten wind of my diet and had hunted me down.

"Who is it?" Julia sang out from across the room where she sat on the floor, back against the couch, legs stretched out towards the puny fire we had somehow managed to keep alive.

A familiar, husky voice called back, "Pizza Man!"

"Patrick?" we silently mouthed to each other. In that neither of us had ordered a pizza, I kept the chain in place and opened the door just a crack to be sure our hunch was correct. There stood my brother, Patrick, the eldest of the 'P's in my family line up of siblings which include Pamela, Phillip, Priscilla and Pairey. I'm thankful that Pairey was my parent's last child, as they were starting to get a little too creative with the naming, if you ask me. I was afraid of ending up with a sibling named Parsnip or Paisley if they had kept it up.

He leaned against the door frame, a large Pizza King box held out like a secret password. Not only were we in need of an upgraded version of junk food, but we had concluded our heavy talk for the evening. I figured we could use the comic relief. I let the pizza in, he followed.

The law of birth order dictates that the eldest be the successful go-getter of the group. If there is to be an overachiever in the family, that distinction usually falls to the eldest. In this, as in most things in his life, Patrick went against the norm. Of the six of us, Patrick had managed to sail through life without *hitting a lick*, as Turner would have said. He only has one credit to his name. He's a great dad to my niece, Carmen. And Carmen is about as good as they come. At age thirteen, she's a talented, well-adjusted kid and loved by all who know her. Patrick had refused to marry Carmen's mother. *Marriage just isn't in my nature.* A reason as ineffectual as knees on bees when a woman is eight-months pregnant. But he was not to be deprived of experiencing the joys of parenthood, so they had decided to live separately and co-parent fifty-fifty. He and Carmen were quite a pair.

He potty trained her, sat through Sesame Street re-runs, and later taught her to read and how to use a boogey board. She was well loved and knew it. In her eyes she had never had a broken home, just two separate residents.

With Carmen, Patrick had finally found a female to whom he could commit. I always secretly felt that if she hadn't come along, he would have ended up a gigolo living off his good looks and charm. For better or worse, he had a way with women and he had, at one time or another, wormed his way into the hearts of half the female population of Hermosa Beach. Didn't matter their age, most women had a secret thing for my brother.

Unfortunately, Julia had been no exception. "Call my brother, Patrick, once you get to L.A.," I had said the day she left Sonoma County. "He'll show you around." And he had. Around his bedroom and around the bend. When they were in their twenties the two had connected like positive and negative poles, like peanut butter and jelly. They couldn't be in each other's presence for more than five minutes without falling into rapture over one another. They moved in together, planned to get married. I had mixed emotions. The thought of welcoming Julia into my family was exciting, but I knew my brother, and of what he was capable. I really didn't wish him on any friend of mine, especially not her. While she was attending Art Academy during the day, he was lazing around on the beach picking up girls. "I've never been so in love!" she told me. I held my breath. By the end of the first year of their co-habitation, Julia moved out, but not before she had attempted suicide by overdosing on sleeping pills.

His antics had singlehandedly undone her. Unfortunately, my brother held the distinction of being the only man aside from her father who had ever rejected her.

Time is our best teacher and heals the deepest of wounds. Some twenty years had passed before Julia could say a civil word to him. It was at my mother's funeral that she agreed to forgive him and put it all behind her. Since then, on the rare occasion when their paths crossed, you'd think they were lifelong buddies.

"Hey Sis," he said, tucking me under his arm. He set the pizza down and with his free hand nuggied the top of my head, my least favorite thing next to tickling. I tried to pull away, but I knew from past experience it was useless to resist. At six-foot-four he towered over me. He was lanky but strong.

"Patrick!" she yelled from her spot on the floor, holding her arms up like a child reaching for daddy.

"How's my girl?" he replied as he sauntered over to her. I could barely believe it but, to my shock, she actually kicked her heels in excitement. He knelt down in front of her and she wrapped her arms around his neck.

"How'd you find us?" I asked, picking off the pepperoni.

"Easy, you left a trail of candy wrappers in your wake," he said, eyeing the empty M&M bag.

I grabbed a couple of napkins and by the time I walked the pizza over to the fireplace, he had Julia sitting on his lap. I perched on the arm of the couch, not knowing exactly where I wanted to sit in this threesome, and sipped champagne while watching the two of them slip effortlessly into flirtatious banter. Julia became more animated and coquettish by the minute.

I know that it's common for women who have been denied love as a child, to have a little girl inside who is forever hanging around ready to pick up crumbs of affection. Nonetheless, I was troubled by the familiarity of the two. Didn't trust it. *And, how did he know we were here anyway?* Although I had every intention of visiting him and Carmen while in the L.A. area, I had planned to do it more toward the end of my trip. Not only did I want Julia all to myself, I didn't feel comfortable with the effect he had on her. It was just too reminiscent of earlier times and I didn't like it.

"Seriously, Patrick, how did you know we were here?" I asked again, this time more directly.

"I phoned him when I got to town yesterday, while I was waiting for you," she explained with a mouth full of pizza. He smiled at the back of her head and began braiding her hair, like I'd seen him do for Carmen.

"Oh?" I said, waiting for more of the story. To which she just nodded her head. They both knew how angry I had been with Patrick for his abhorrent treatment of her in the past. They both knew how I had supported her decision to be done with him for good. Hell, to get through her *farewell forever* speech, she had to write it down, memorize it and deliver it as a monologue to keep her heart from breaking. In her usual fashion she had gotten a bit carried away and had turned it into community theater, calling him a narcissistic worm of a man, adding in some derogatory comments about his penis and ending it with her finger pointing to the heavens and decreeing like some goddess scorned, "There shall be no mercy for you!"

To this day Patrick claims that the reason he never married is because he could never find anyone like Julia, and she was smart enough not to have him. As far as I knew, once she'd made up her mind to leave him behind she hadn't given him another thought. I hoped I hadn't been naive all these years. They sure looked chummy.

Julia's asking, "How's Carmen?" was sufficient prompting to launch him into a sweet and funny tale of Carmen as *The Little Mermaid* in her school's play. In less than a minute he had Julia doubling over with laughter. I helped myself to another slice of pizza and allowed my big brother to sweep me up in his storytelling ability. *Relax,* I told myself, *take a break. Don't analyze everything.*

I slid off the couch, joining the two of them on the floor and before too long was caught up in the joy of family and friendship at its best. We toasted to Carmen. We ate, drank and laughed until we were no longer able. I considered myself fortunate to be sitting before a fire in a room overlooking Malibu Beach with pizza, my favorite sibling and my long lost and dearest friend. Whatever was to happen tomorrow or the next day, we'd handle then. Tonight I had my arms around Julia and Patrick and nothing else mattered.

## *Shelly:*

It had been four days. It would be five before it was over, all due to the long weekend and some legal technicality. He droned on and on. How sorry he was, and if he could only take it all back. Blah, blah, blah. The worst of it was he had brought Samantha with him. Now she'd have this wonderful memory of her mother behind a glass partition, no makeup, grey jumpsuit with guard standing by.

He could talk all he wanted. She had nothing to say to him. Her only concern was finding the right words and tone of voice to soothe her five-yr-old daughter who kept craning around in her chair, her eyes wide with disbelief, saying "Mommy? Mommy?"

"Sweetheart, Samantha, look at Mommy now. Right here baby." She touched the glass that separated the small hand from her own. "I'll be home tomorrow afternoon after nap time, OK?"

"Mommy, come home with us now!" she whined, her head dropping to the cold metal table in front of her.

"Samantha, look at Mommy, Sweetie."

She raised her head, her pale skin splotchy with distress. Shelly saw herself there in her little girl, and anger welled up inside her. She swore her children would have a better life than she had, and look. *That bastard!* She couldn't take it anymore. She couldn't stand the frantic look on Samantha's face.

"Mommy loves you baby," she said rising. The guard stood to return her to her cell. She didn't have the courage to look back. Had she, she would have seen her daughter's thin arms outstretched, her husband blubbering his apologies.

Four days prior, a day like any other, a day of sneaking around, plotting, trying to get out of a situation that was only bound to get worse with time, Shelly had carefully removed the chipped mirror from over the wash basin. Nervous, she fumbled with the silver duct tape. *Thank God his mother called. He'll be distracted for awhile. Scissors, where are the scissors?* She tore off a piece with her teeth, then another. She could hear Daimon banging his cup and yelling for juice. The video *Snow White* could be heard through the bathroom door. That meant Samantha would be sitting two feet from the tube mouthing the words that had become familiar to her after watching it about thirty times. They only had a few kid videos. Flat out couldn't afford them. Hell, could barely afford the juice that Daimon was now screaming for. *I hate living like this.*

She could hear Daryl hang up the phone in the kitchen. "All right, all right, here's your juice," he said, irritated by the interruption. She turned on the shower, made sure for the third time that the door was locked, and taping the letter securely to the back of the mirror, hung it back over the sink. She tested it, making sure it would under no circumstances fall off, prematurely revealing her plan.

"Shelly," he bellowed, standing in front of a fridge containing a pitcher of Hawaiian Punch, half a quart of milk, a white box with the large black letters OATMEAL on it and nothing else—indicating it was from the food shelter—an economy-size jar of peanut butter (generic), some saltines, three rotting apples and a handful of wilted spinach in the crisper. Shelly kept her breads and grains in the fridge, away from the small insects that had taken up permanent residence in the six-by-eight cubby hole the owner called a kitchenette. Daryl opened the freezer compartment and wondered at the brown tubular shape solidly encased in a block of ice that had grown to take over the small freezer. He slammed the door and sauntered over to the bathroom. From outside the door he could hear the shower running. He knew from past experience that the water running didn't necessarily indicate she was bathing. She had used that tactic before when she just wanted to be alone, when she didn't want him bothering her. He hated that.

"Hey," he banged on the door. "Open up."

"Daryl, I'm trying to get ready for work," she called back.

"Open!" he demanded, banging again, "I have to piss." He chuckled to himself. He didn't really have to piss, he just didn't like locked doors.

"Go pee in the yard," came the reply.

He pressed his ear to the door and from the sounds he could tell the shower noise was nothing more than a diversion, as he had expected. "I said open the damn door!"

Shelly held her breath. Minutes passed and finally when she heard the garage door open she figured he'd given up. She finished putting on her eyeliner, then took two steps back to get a better look at herself, take inventory. Tummy too poochy, breasts too saggy, hips too wide. *Well, the kids are worth it.* She sighed and began brushing out her tangled hair. Anyone looking at her would have judged her more kindly. *All you need is a little toning,* Julia had said. *Stop drinking so much and lay off all those hot dogs.* The steam from the shower was beginning to fog the mirror, making the imperfections more difficult to detect. She heard Daryl at the door again. She leaned over the sink, defeat a heavy weight to carry.

She wished she could dissolve as easily as her reflection, enveloped in a soft haze and magically transported into some other life. Daryl never hesitated to point out her shortcomings. "*Hey Lard Ass, what's for dinner?*" he'd say as a form of greeting when she returned home from work. Angry with herself for taking his crap for so long, she began yanking the brush through her hair. If she needed yet another reason for leaving him, the bit with Laura had been the topper. *As if I care where you stick that puny excuse for a penis.*

She wiped the mirror, and leaning over to turn off the shower water, heard the familiar sound of the door latch being picked. *Not again! Damn him!* She grabbed the knob in an attempt to steady the latch. The screwdriver and his strength overpowered her easily. He burst through the door, banging her head in the process.

"You have no right to do this!" she yelled, "I'm entitled to some privacy around here! Don't forget, we are getting a divorce you know." She lowered her voice when she said the word divorce. It was hard to know what words were known by children raised on TV.

"Yeah, yeah. Nothing final yet. And til it is, it's not over til it's over. I do what I want, when I want," he said smuggly. "Understand?" he thumped the nipple of her left breast like it was a fly at a picnic table.

"Don't you touch me," she said through clenched teeth. She backed up against the sink, her thoughts shifting momentarily to the mirror and its hidden document—her salvation. He pressed up against her, his stale breath and body odor revolting, making her stomach heave.

He thumped the other nipple. "I do what I want."

She spit in his face. "Get out!"

He grabbed a handful of her hair and yanked her head back, slamming it into the wall once, twice. She momentarily slipped into another place. A place where a teenage Shelly stood helpless while Nora, a handful of hair in each fist, slammed her head into the kitchen wall. *You-Do-As-You're-Told*, a slam for each word. The room came into focus again as he let go and stood back looking at her with menace and disgust. Her well-honed survival instincts took over. She said nothing, eyes down and feigning defeat, turned back toward the sink. Leaning over she got her balance just right and in one unexpected, unplanned movement, delivered one swift side kick to his genitals, like some kind of kung-fu chick. He doubled over gasping and grabbing his crotch.

"I hate you, I hate you, I hate you," she screamed as she beat him with her wire hairbrush.

From the kitchen, Daimon banged his juice cup. Samantha, still wearing her Winnie-the-Pooh jammies, stood at the end of the hall, hands cupping her ears, shouting "No, Mommy, stop! Mommy stop!"

When Samantha's voice reached her, Shelly came to her senses, and thinking Daryl momentarily subdued, ran to the bedroom to throw on some clothes. She was in the process of struggling with the zipper of her jeans, when he hit her from behind. He grabbed her arm and spun her around.

"Look at this," he shouted, showing her the welts that had begun to form on his back. "Spousal abuse!"

"Yeah, right," she said, trying to jerk her arm back.

A smirk slid across his face as he dragged her over to the phone in the kitchen. He pinned her against the wall, and to her amazement, dialed 911. She stayed pinned to the wall, watching his welts rise and redden, as the Santa Rosa police rushed to his rescue.

* * *

**The few days she spent in jail** weren't without benefit. For starters she wasn't allowed any alcohol, and by day three she realized she wasn't waking up every morning with her head fogged. *Maybe I really do need to lay off.* It would be tough while she was still living with Daryl. She'd been trying to numb herself out for so many years she had lost track of the insidious toll her drinking had taken on her body and state of mind. But things were about to change. The letter from the Housing Authority that was still hiding behind the bathroom mirror informed her that she indeed was eligible for assisted housing and due to her two children and the threat of violence in the home, her name had been placed near the top of the list.

She closed her eyes, slowed her breathing and tried the visualization technique Julia had taught her. She imagined the three of them snug and safe cuddled up together in their new bedroom that overlooked a beautiful garden. She saw her children playing in the yard, joyfully chasing butterflies, while she looked on from the kitchen window where she prepared a nutritious meal. Everything in her new home was clean and orderly, tranquil and calm.

"Lunch!" the guard bellowed, as he brought her tray in and placed it next to her on the cot that had been her bed for the last four days. The food was an unappetizing slop of browns and grays. It was impossible to tell which food group they belonged without actually tasting them. She wasn't that curious. She opted for the carton of milk. *This might not be so bad after all. A little peace and quiet to get my life sorted out, and I might even drop a few pounds. I'm beginning to sound like Julia.* She chuckled to herself and hoped that Paula was right, that Julia would be home soon. As the guard locked the door to her cell he glanced at Shelly in a way that brought back a memory of other lockups, of Lucky—her mother's San Quentin sweetie.

* * *

**Nora had somehow managed** to convince herself that she had found the love of her life behind the walls of San Quentin, and had delusions of becoming Mrs. Lucky, happily ever-aftering once he was out. Lucky, of course, did nothing to discourage her line of thought—played it up, in fact. Nora took Shelly with her on numerous visitations so she could bond with Daddy Lucky.

"Yuk!" Shelly exclaimed a bit too loudly, at the memory of being forced to call that sleezeball, Daddy.

"Yeah, yeah. But that's all you get. Might as well eat up," the guard said as he passed by her cell, mistaking her outburst to be the usual commentary on the food.

It didn't take Lucky long to figure out he had a mullet on the line. He had Nora sneaking him contraband, making phone calls on his behalf and eventually he even convinced her to play a role in Lucky's Great Escape. Six months into their romance he was transferred to a minimal security prison a few hours south of the Bay Area. Together they plotted and finally hatched a scheme wherein on a particular night at a certain time Nora and her car were to show up at a specific Texaco station. The gas station would naturally be closed that late at night. After his escape, he explained carefully, he would have quite a trek through the hills to keep out of sight, but he admonished her to hang tight and not split on him if he didn't arrive at the Texaco exactly when he said he would.

On the designated evening, Nora loaded Shelly, three chicken sandwiches and a gallon jug of Gallo red table wine into her '62 Chevy and off they went to rescue Lucky. Nora's sense of direction had never been terrific, nor was she the best choice for a getaway driver, but she was all Lucky had. She did the best she could to follow his directives, but in the end she got flustered and knocked off course when she missed a turn. She could justify anything, so she blithely convinced herself that he must have been mistaken about the actual name of the gas station and pulled into an abandoned Conoco station some two miles from the Texaco where she was suppose to be.

While Shelly occupied herself in the back seat with her doll and coloring books, Nora settled in with her jug wine and her dreams of the new life she would have with Lucky. He had misled her into believing that he had a stash of solid gold crucifixes in a safe-deposit box in Nevada and that they'd be sitting pretty once the crucifixes had been melted down and sold as bullion. That night wasn't the first time Lucky hadn't lived up to his name.

His escape had been easy compared to his hike across the hills to the Texaco. And everything had gone according to plan until he arrived at the gas station and saw she wasn't there. He tried to dismiss the sinking feel that crept over him by telling himself that she was just late, as usual. He couldn't very well hang around the station and draw attention to himself, so he hid out in the hills, checking back throughout the night. By three in the morning Nora was plastered, sound asleep with mouth-wide-open snores and a half-eaten chicken sandwich in her lap. And that's how she stayed, with Shelly sleeping curled up in the backseat, until six a.m. when a police officer knocked on her window.

To her credit she managed to make her situation appear to be perfectly ordinary—too tired to drive—can't drink while driving, ya know. Yada, yada, yada. As they left the station to return home they drove by the Texaco where they should have been waiting. Nora, realizing the magnitude of her error, spent the whole of the drive back rehearsing her excuses. She was so focused on her alibi that she failed to see Lucky hitchhiking on the other side of the road. But he saw her. *Dumb Bitch!*

Lucky stayed at Nora's for two days before he hit the road. He said that her house would be the first place the authorities looked for him and he'd be back for her and Shelly once he had reclaimed the crosses. It didn't take an eight-year-old to figure out that he had been using her from the start. And although she had been a decent enough lay for a guy that hadn't had any in four years, he quickly discovered that she was not the cute little dish he'd been led to believe. She had failed to mention the fact that breast cancer had claimed her right breast the year prior—a startling discovery to make in the heat of the moment—especially since she had been parading around San Quentin in low cut pushed-up and padded bras. False advertising in Lucky's book.

Then there was the matter of her snoring. If he was going to get any sleep at all he'd have to get out of there. So what if he had been touched by the song she wrote him? It was a song about him being a bird set free to fly to the nest of his one true love, and he did feel like a bird, sort of. But true to form, she had wrecked it, as far as he was concerned, by playing an imaginary keyboard on the kitchen table for accompaniment. Maybe she could hear something, but he couldn't and he'd be damned if he was going to spend his life with a delusional one-tit broad that couldn't even afford a second-hand upright. That was the last they ever saw of Daddy Lucky.

# *Paula:*

A week had passed since Pizza With Patrick. I had originally thought that we'd spend the full two weeks in fairly typical therapy sessions, interspersed with time-outs for meals and toilet breaks. But after that evening, I revised our game plan, realizing that it would be better if we just mixed it up a bit, pretend that we're two old friends on vacation, complete with lunches and walks on the beach, that are sprinkled liberally with hard hitting questions of a leading nature. I came to this decision after trying it the more traditional way and finding her resistant. It was difficult to pin her down. As much as she wanted to deal with the issues of her past, it was more comfortable for her to skirt the topics I presented, choosing instead to hide in concepts. And to be completely accurate, we were involved in a sort of role reversal, and I for one, found it a bit challenging.

One thing was certain. The evening she spent with Patrick and I cheered her up more than I would have expected. She was downright chirpy. And she was obviously pleased that, since that night, he had been checking in every day. As much as I was relieved to see some of the old Julia back, I was a bit irritated that our days together were zooming by and I was having a difficult time approaching the more vulnerable side she had exposed before Patrick's arrival. She was slippery and I was going to have to sharpen up if we were to make headway.

"I've always felt directed," she said, taking an unexpected right-hand turn. We were on our way to lunch at Randolph's. Had I been driving we would have continued on straight ahead for another half mile before turning off the main road. I said nothing, knowing that we'd get there eventually and not wanting to interrupt the flow of her thoughts. I had learned over the years not to question her meanderings—either of thought or of auto—for things usually turned out OK, the point or the destination being reached sooner or later.

"I've learned to trust my intuition and just be spontaneous with life. That's where most people get bogged down. They just think things to death," she said as we bounced our way through a construction zone. "They refuse to let life hold any mystery for them. Everything is planned out in advance." Her Miata bottomed out in a pot hole. "Nothing left to chance."

A young boy on roller blades momentarily lost his balance, as we watched him swing around a bus stop sign at the intersection we were approaching. He steadied himself, then as the light changed he skated off the curb and landed plunk on his fanny a few feet into the crosswalk. We smiled at each other as we cautiously skirted around him.

"You know," she went on, "only young kids really know what they want. Unlike adults who syphon every bit of information through the filter of years and the neuronal synapses that are woven into and around every event, regardless of how insignificant. 'Shall I get out of bed?' we ask ourselves, and the brain springs into action supplying reams of data based on previous experience and precedents. Our cerebral computers, sophisticated as they are, not only run through our emotional software to guide us, but call out sensorial reckonings, like tactile sensations, aromas and creative visuals to guide our decision making process. It's no wonder spontaneity slips through our fingers the more seasoned we become. Hmm," she mused, "seasoned, an interesting word to describe the latter years. Our seasoning depends on the current life recipe we've chosen."

"Personally, I would have preferred a little more lemon zest," I offered.

"There you go!" she said nodding her approval. "And Shelly, for example, could have done with a lot less pepper."

"Or maybe some turbinado."

"No, she's sweet enough, it's just her temper that gets her, her inner rage."

I thought of my last phone conversation with Shelly. I had to agree about the pepper.

"You get my point anyway. Most people have allowed themselves only a bland diet and stick to it regardless of the feasting going on all around them."

"You sound like Auntie Mame."

She laughed, "I don't mean to pontificate here Paula, just trying to help you understand why I'm usually comfortable trusting life to reveal itself to me, rather than trying to hogtie it into some preconceived and probably shortsighted vision."

This topic of conversation had started by my suggesting she call off this make-believe wedding that was rapidly approaching, due to the simple fact that there was no groom. How we made our way from there to discussing condiments was typical of how she was manipulating our conversations in order to avoid dealing with some key issues. I could tell I was going to have to get tough. I figured over lunch would be the right time, but first I wanted to get her impression of my current non-existent love life.

"Take my life for example," I offered. "I've always had a plan and I've worked the plan. So far my life *looks* pretty good, on paper, anyway. But I wouldn't say I'm thrilled with how my life *feels.* I'm forty-seven years old, have a great practice, my finances are in order, I'm in good shape and am reasonably attractive . . ." I paused a half-beat to give her an opportunity to chime in, like I knew she would.

"No, not reasonably attractive. You're a knockout. I can't go anywhere with you without being subjected to drooling males."

"Well, I am fortunate to have splashed down into a fairly handsome gene pool.

"I'll say."

"But all-in-all my life is pretty predictable, not real exciting. I've dotted every 'i' that's come my way, crossed every 't', imagining that if

I stayed on top of it, life would just naturally be beautiful. Instead it's kind of flat. I haven't even had a date with anyone interesting in over a year.

"Really? That's amazing, Paula. I guess that's what comes from all that 'i' dotting. You've kept yourself in such a tight framework that there's not been anywhere in your life where the universe can respond. Sometimes it's best to just turn it over to the cosmos and trust, really trust, that everything is unfolding for your highest good. Once you come to that point, all the things that seem lose-ended and unsettling can be seen from a different perspective. After all, everyone of us is living the life of our own choosing. We've selected our personal set of circumstances so that we can learn from our experiences and evolve spiritually."

Her philosophy of life was not unfamiliar to me. I did note that she had refined her thinking since our college days, as one would expect. I was eager to learn how she justified her philosophy with her current state of restlessness and her nightly apartment shopping.

We pulled into the popular seaside restaurant. It was packed as usual, and judging by all the cars I knew we would have to wait for a table. Once in the lot, Julia turned into the first parking spot she saw, never mind that it was half a block from the entrance. "Don't you believe in manifesting parking spots?" I said, blending in another application of sun screen. I was determined to march into my latter years spotless. I can't stand those blotchy brown stains women get on their hands and face. I hadn't taken meticulous care of my skin all my life to stop now.

"Nah," she replied. "I save up for bigger things."

"Most people I know would have driven around for ten minutes trying to avoid walking fifty feet."

"I know, and just think of all the great tables they'd let slip by while they're out here circling," she said with a wink. We walked through the front door and there it was, all ready for us, our table for two overlooking the water, with us the only party of two in sight.

"How about that one over there?" I pointed to the table. The waiter nodded and escorted us to our seats.

"Maybe I'll take up roller blading," she said as we gazed out at a perfect California day.

"Why not surfing while you're at it, or hang gliding? You should have thought of roller blading ten years ago, your bones would have had a chance. Julia, you're 52 years old, haven't you heard of osteoporosis?"

"Seems I have," she said ignoring me, and perusing the menu.

"Besides, with your roaming nature I don't want to see the headline *Northern California Senior Airlifted Out of Some Inaccessible Spot After Breaking Leg while on Some Roller Blading Trek Across the Himalayas* I said sweeping my hand across an imaginary newspaper that hung in the air between us. Her laughter kept me going, and we sat there dreaming up other impossible situations with headlines to match. The more absurd, the more we laughed. Somehow we managed to calm down by the time the waiter arrived to take our order.

“OK Julia,” I said reaching for the Equal to put in my ice tea, “tell me more.”

“Where were we?”

“It doesn’t matter. Just close your eyes a minute and see what memory springs forward.” I’ve learned over the years that with people like Julia there are usually visions lined up in their psyche patiently awaiting their summons, one behind the other and all ready to march forward, given the opportunity and the right set of circumstances.

Her eyes were closed for about half a nanosecond when she said “Cell phone.”

*Cell phone?* I quickly scanned my memory bank to see if there had ever been a deposit made under the category Julia and the Cell Phone. Then I remembered, and knew we were heading into avalanche territory. Her eyes remained closed, her body was as still as death. When she found her voice it was thin and brittle. “Turner,” she croaked. It might not have been the best place to go into a subject that was packed with such high emotion, but I’d take what I could get.

Somewhere in the China Sea a little boy skipped a stone at water’s edge, which started a ripple, which turned into a wave, which found its way to the California coastline. It broke in a thunder outside our window right about the time the vichyssoise was served. By then, she was ready to talk.

“We’d had a fight the night before. A stupid fight. Can you guess what about?” she asked, buttering a piece of sourdough.

"No," I replied.

"My coming to visit you."

"Me? Why would you fight about that?"

"I guess it was the way I approached the subject."

"Approach? You had to approach the topic of visiting your best friend? Why didn't you just inform him you were going?"

"That's exactly what I did. I should have known better."

I resisted the urge to roll my eyes. I would never ask permission for something as innocent and natural as visiting an old friend. But then again, I'd never been married. It was difficult for me to imagine Julia asking permission.

"Turner didn't like my being away from him, ever, for any reason. For all his strength, my absence seemed to threaten him somehow." She picked at her food. "He just had this overwhelming need to always be in charge, never to be questioned or second guessed. I allowed him his role. Most of the areas where he required compliance were not all that important to me anyway. I can't get too worked up over little stuff, but he sure could, so I thought if I could go along and still be in a loving space about it, not harboring resentments, I'd comply. That's why I dressed the way he wanted me to, kept the house immaculate, even tried to take up golf. Now that was a disaster!"

"I can just see it." And I could: Julia in flowing skirts dancing around the uncooperative ball, laughing, then picking it up and dropping it in the hole.

She held up her right thumb. "Sprained my thumb smacking the ground so many times. The game is just too rigid for my taste. Has all these rules."

"And where does the cell phone come in?" I asked, trying to gently steer her back to the topic at hand. *If I were her, I'd try to avoid it too.*

"Like I was saying, for the sake of harmony, I'd allow Turner to call the shots. Something I'd never done before; too scarey, you know." I could feel her tapping the leg of the table with her foot. "Whenever I made my own decisions and acted independently he thought I was running amuck. If he wasn't at the helm, his world wasn't a safe place."

"That must have been quite a sacrifice on your part, Julia. I had no idea."

"Well, harmony's my game, you know. I loved him and I trusted his judgment. I knew he loved me, and I also knew he didn't have a mean bone in his body. It was just that . . ." She put her fork down, sighed deeply, ". . . he saw the world in black and white—no grays allowed. He had very set ideas on how the world operated."

"I assume that included your role in his world?"

"Yes. Very definitely. He tried to squeeze me into one too many boxes and that particular evening I just lost it. Told him he could go to hell. Screamed, smashed our wedding photo and stormed out of the house. Big, ugly scene." I knew her well enough to know that it would have taken a lot to get her to that point.

"I had lived for so many years under my mother's tyranny . . ." She choked up.

We sat in silence, sipped our tea. "When I got back later that night, he was already asleep and I was still mad, so I slept downstairs in the guest bedroom. I wasn't sure how he was going to respond to my outburst, but I knew whatever was coming, it would be watered down by the time morning rolled around. So when I woke up, I put on the coffee, thumbed through a few magazines while I waited for him to wake and come down to breakfast. I was prepared to deal with our differences calmly. I was all set to present my case in a way that would hopefully make sense to him. I fully expected to be able to win him over, have the light finally dawn on him. *'Oh, you meant spend a week visiting Paula! I see, of course Sweetheart. Have a good time.'* "She stirred the ice cubes in her tea with her index finger.

"What happened?"

"He never came down to breakfast. So at ten o'clock I went upstairs to our room to see if he was still sleeping, and if not, to try and make it right."

She stopped breathing again.

"And?"

"He wasn't there. He had left the house that morning before I even woke up." She stared out across the Pacific. "That's where the cell phone comes in."

Now I remembered. I just hadn't been aware of the lead-in to the story.

"I called him and he answered." Tears spilled onto her salad.

"Yes," I said, reaching across the table to cover her hand with my own.

"Paula, he answered his cell phone while riding his Harley."

I knew the rest of the story by heart, but this was no time to remind her.

"He answered the call, saying he thought it might be me. I said 'Turner, where are you? What's that noise? Are you on your Harley?' He could barely hear me, kept yelling 'What? Speak louder.' I said, 'Turner, I'm hanging up. You can't talk on a cell and safely operate a motorcycle. You'll crash.'"

I shifted over to the seat next to her so I could cradle her head while she cried. When she caught her breath, she continued. "The police report said that he had cut the curve too sharply, had lost control of his bike and had skidded across two lanes of traffic before he . . . before his bike . . ."

"I know, Sweetie. Julia, it wasn't your fault."

"I shouldn't have called."

"It wasn't your fault."

"I shouldn't have argued."

"It wasn't your fault."

"I should have said absolutely no Harleys. You know how I feel about them."

"It wasn't your fault."

"I never should have slept in the guest bedroom."

"It's not your fault."

She wiped her face with the backs of her hands and looked me straight in the eye and said, "I never should have said 'You'll crash.'"

All the cards were stacked on the table and it was my turn to deal. We'd had our walks on the beach and we'd had play time. We'd done some serious work in some very public places. Although we had covered a lot of ground, I knew there was more. Four days before we left Malibu I insisted we have some concentrated therapy time.

"I was wondering when we were going to get around to that!" she said jokingly. I selected EMDR therapy as my weapon of choice to do battle with her more painful memories. Eye Movement Desensitization and Reprocessing is a process wherein the therapist induces rapid eye movement in a client by holding her fingers about eighteen inches from the client's face and moving them back and forth like a windshield wiper. The client, while recalling a traumatic memory, tracks the movement with her eyes, which stimulates the two hemispheres of the brain to communicate with each other, thus revealing a fresh way to interpret a past traumatic experience. This form of therapy has been gaining in popularity since the initial medical study in 1989 which showed positive therapeutic results, especially with trauma victims. It is a rather simple therapy, but one that can bring quick and lasting relief for most types of emotional distress. It is similar to the rapid eye movement we experience while dreaming which helps us diffuse and discharge the events of the day.

That's why things generally look better in the morning. That's why we *sleep on it.* The end result is a sort of neurological reprogramming. Although the memory may still be painful, it's not as painful, and it loses its grip on the psyche, allowing the client to move beyond the event and hopefully move forward in her life. Once someone has been able to relive an incident with induced rapid eye movement, we can then ask that person's subconscious mind to provide helpful images to assist with the reprogramming.

Thankfully, Julia was easily directed in this manner and seemed to enjoy the process, so we spent many hours tidying up her life a bit. Underlying a lot of her pain was her fear that she had in some way failed in her marriage, and more significantly and irrationally, that she was responsible for Turner's death. While I induced rapid eye movement, I had her re-live her last phone conversation with Turner. It was painful to watch her dip into that memory, but I knew that her inner strength and the subconscious workings of her mind would guide her to an image of their time together that she could hold onto. It took some time, but when it was all said and done she came away knowing that her relationship with Turner, short as it was, had been a success. I pointed out that when confronted with the dictates of a demanding, controlling husband, she had not lost herself. Where she had bent, she had done so lovingly; and where she could not bend, she had stood up for herself. All things considered, a healthy approach. Throughout their relationship and in spite of their differences, they had still managed to have a happy marriage.

The fact that Turner's controlling nature reminded her of her mother was something that was acknowledged, although she elected to defer further discussion of her childhood until a later date, maintaining that she felt lighter and ready to get on with her life. I had to admit that she appeared relieved and more relaxed. I considered the therapy successful, as far as it went; I knew we weren't through yet. I also knew that Julia would not be pushed. It was time to leave Malibu and the sanctuary it afforded. I would have to be patient.

* * *

I arranged to spend some time with Carmen the Friday before Julia and I left for Sonoma. My niece got to choose how we would spend our day together. I had been expecting a day at the beach, maybe a movie, some shopping. Aunties are always good for a new outfit, especially Aunties that live out of town. Instead we ended up in Anaheim, for a jam-packed, whirlwind day at Disneyland. Carmen wouldn't go on a single ride unless I joined her so, scaredy cat that I am, I made myself bite the bullet and somehow managed to survive the day.

Needless to say, I returned to Malibu later than I had imagined, giving Julia and Patrick a full day in each other's company. I tried not to show my surprise when she announced her plans for the day. I had envisioned her taking the opportunity to have some time alone to process the work we had done, perhaps write in her journal or something else reflective in nature. A day spent strolling the trails in Topanga Canyon with Patrick just sounded a little too sexy to suit me. I told myself to let go of it. I knew I was being over protective, but I flat out couldn't imagine any good springing from the two of them alone in the woods together.

Rather than obsess, I allowed myself to be distracted by my adorable niece and the little-girl events that make up her life. With her spending money she purchased the latest Disney invention, a key chain with an animated hologram of a miniature Carmen encased in Lucite that mouthed the words "I love you Dad" and blew a kiss. Five o'clock rolled around before we knew it. Sticky with cotton candy, full of Coke and fashionably attired in Mickey Mouse ears, we loaded into the car and assumed our rightful place in rush hour madness. Although it had been a year since I had seen her, by the time I dropped her off at her mom's in Redondo Beach we were as close as ever.

"Bye Love," I said as she wrapped her arms around my waist.

"Bye Aunt Paula," she said smiling up at me with that clear, uncluttered gaze of a child. "Can I really come up for Spring Break?"

"Of course you can! But to be on the safe side, better get clearance from your parental governing bodies. As far as I'm concerned, it's a done deal."

"Oh goodie!" She clapped her hands and turned to go inside. Halfway up the walk, she turned back. "Will Julia be there?"

"I think that's the plan."

"Then she's not moving back down here?"

"No. What would give you that idea?"

"I don't know. Bye Aunt Paula."

"Carmen? Why did you ask me that?"

"Um . . . I guess I misunderstood. I heard Dad say something like that on the phone."

*It's none of my business. It is none of my business. It's none of my business.* I had to remind myself nearly every hour. *She's a grown woman. She knows what he's like.* It must have shown on my face, my disappointment, but I couldn't help myself, especially since she found it necessary to recall in great detail the cute little vignettes of their day together. Anyone listening would have thought Patrick the wittiest and most charming of men.

Now, after what Carmen had said about Julia moving to L.A., everything she said about Patrick was suspect. Frankly I couldn't imagine her leaving Sonoma County for Los Angeles for any reason, much less my ne'er-do-well brother. Still, it did set me to thinking about the two of them, about the bond they've always had. *It's none of my business.*

"Julia?"

"Hmm?" she said absentmindedly as she hoisted my suitcase into the trunk of my Volvo.

"You'd never consider hooking up with Patrick again, would you?" *It's none of my business.*

"Paula," she said straightening up, hands on hips, "you worry too much." Not the response for which I was hoping, but she was right nonetheless. I did worry too much. I knew that about myself. It was likely this very fact contributed significantly to my status as a single woman. Whenever I met someone I cared for, I'd start right in worrying. First, I'd worry that he wouldn't like me; then when he did, I'd worry that he didn't like me for the right reasons. Next, I'd worry that he wouldn't call; then when he did, I'd worry that he could sense my worry. Once we started going out it was time to start worrying about the size of my breasts. If he managed to convince me they were fine, then I'd move on to worrying about areas where I might not be fine. Surely I wasn't fine in some way, because men were always leaving me.

Once I had sufficiently worried about my probable shortcomings, I'd start in on his. I'd worry that he wasn't eating right; didn't exercise enough; that his job was going nowhere; that he spent too much time on the phone with his Ex, and that his devotion to Marilyn Manson couched unresolved oedipal leanings. In essence, I worried him right out the door. I'm a bright woman. I can see what I'm doing while I'm in the process of doing it, I just can't stop myself.

Then there was my best friend, the one who *should* be worrying. The one heading into a wedding with no husband, whistling a cheery little tune and trusting the cosmos to provide, direct and protect her. I wish I could have mastered that. My life might look different right now if I had kept an eye out for the signs along the way, the winks and nods from the universe. In Julia I have a master teacher. All I need do is pay attention.

* * *

**We left Malibu reluctantly.** I had to return to my practice. I was beginning to worry that I'd been gone too long, knowing full well that my clients with abandonment issues were not appreciating my absence. And Julia had to return to the life she had run from. There were situations awaiting her which would be difficult for her to face. Our time together had been precious to me, and it was comforting to know the feeling was mutual. I knew that I had helped her, and I was grateful for the opportunity to do so. I could see the effect of it on her already. She was springier. She practically bounced as she walked, her hair swinging from side to side, like a young girl on her way to cheerleading camp. I wished all my clients had the capacity to respond as quickly as she had. I just hoped I wasn't fooling myself about the reason for the bounce in her step.

Try as I might I couldn't quite come to terms with the fact that she hadn't canceled the wedding. Instead, once we arrived back home, she began calling caterers. First on her list was Patisserie Angelica on Mendocino Avenue. I knew the bakery well and couldn't blame her. The wedding cakes in the window are works of art and a good enough reason for any woman to want to get married.

"Julia, this is crazy. Just call it off!" I cried. I wanted to spare her the embarrassment that was sure to follow.

"Oh ye of little faith" she'd quote, and continue dialing.

"But how do you *feel* about all this?" I asked, as floral designers lined up to show off their portfolios.

She looked me squarely in the eye and said, "Well, I'm excited."

"But you don't have a groom. No fiancé. Not even a date for Saturday night."

"I know. I know. Calm down. It's all going to work out."

"How is it going to work out? Answer me that. How is everything going to work out?" I could feel myself getting exasperated with her casual attitude.

"La Señora was very certain about this."

"Who's this La Señora person?"

"Oh, never mind. I just have to go with the flow on this, Paula."

"Well, I must say, you have got quite a *flow* going on around here," I said sweeping my arm around her bedroom, which was strewn with books and fabric swatches. I shook my head, paced and sulked until my controlling nature took over. In spite of myself I couldn't help but get caught up in the planning of the event.

"What about the cold?"

"Cold?" she responded as if hearing the word for the first time.

"Oh, you know, Cold. December. Northern California," I said, making a rolling gesture with my hand, hoping she'd catch on to the concept I was trying to convey. "Evening. The Beach. The word *Cold* just naturally follows."

"Hmm. Of course. You're right." She was silent for a moment. Wheels were turning. "I'll take care of it," she announced. I sighed and plunked down on her bed amidst a pile of shimmery fabric.

"Now Paula . . ."

"I know. I worry too much." Secretly I hoped she'd ask me to be her maid or matron of honor, whatever it is you are when you're the best woman. I had never been asked to be in a wedding party, let alone be a maid. As ridiculous as it seemed, that very fact made me feel like I had missed out on something crucial to womanhood. It felt like being the last one picked when choosing up sides for kick ball. I couldn't help but just spit it out: "Are you planning on having a wedding party?" I asked, surprising myself by swinging my feet back and forth off the edge of the bed like I use to do when I was five and wanted permission to spend the night at Susie's.

"No. Too old for that. I can stand up by myself."

*Robbed again.* I stopped swinging my feet, a gesture that did not go unnoticed.

"But Paula, if you'd feel more included, we can . . ."

"No No. That's not necessary, really!" I objected strenuously to cover for my vulnerability. Most of us therapists didn't get there by accident I reminded myself. *So I'm a bit insecure. So what?* In the middle of my reassuring her that I was fine with her decision to exclude me, once again, from her wedding plans, the phone rang. As it was resting on the bed next to me I picked it up on the first ring. "Party central," I said in a deadpan voice.

"Hey Sis."

"Patrick?"

"Yeah, how's my favorite little snuggle bunny?"

"I'm great. How did you know I was here?"

"Didn't. I'm calling for Julia."

"Oh, OK. Hang on."

"Hey! Not so fast."

"What?"

"I miss you."

"I was just there."

"I know. I just didn't realize how good it felt having you close by. Carmen misses you too."

“Patrick, you sweet talker. Here’s Julia,” I said, handing off the receiver.

“Patrick!” She was over-joyed to get his call. She strolled off with the phone to talk in private. I didn’t realize he had her number. I was certain they hadn’t been in contact until just recently. Years had passed without them seeing or speaking to one another; now all of a sudden . . . *it’s none of my business.* I caught a fleeting glimpse of her twirling a strand of hair as she paced back and forth outside on the back deck, her laughter filtering through the french doors.

I have to admit to being a tad jealous. For all his faults I really do like my brother and I love basking in the glow of his attention. Patrick had been my guiding light in my youth. He was a loving brother who never made me feel like an interloper whenever he was with his guy friends. I could tell he was proud of me, by the way he introduced me. I was his favorite sibling. Still am.

He’s the one who got me interested in running, taught me how to backpack, hike and camp. He knows everything there is to know about the outdoors. He’d make up stories about the stars overhead to entertain me around the campfire, inventing constellations and mythological characters to suit his tales. With his quick and creative mind, he was a master storyteller. If I could convince myself to overlook his irresponsible ways, I had to admit, I missed him too.

## *Shelly:*

The knot in my stomach, having used up all available space, began creeping up my esophagus to its final resting place in my throat. I had to swallow three times to lubricate my vocal cords to the point where they would actually work when called upon.

When she finally came to the door, I took one look at her face and felt like the VCR had been taken off "pause" and my life could pick up again. The two years of her absence had left me feeling abandoned and unable to steer a clear course through the obstacles of my life. I needed my sister to show me where to plant my feet so that the ground didn't shift so.

Just when I thought I'd commence our reunion by spilling tears, longing and pain all over her marble entry, I found my voice and was able to croak out a feeble, "I'm so glad you're home," as she folded me into her, stroking my hair and rocking me until I could breathe normally again.

Samantha, who had been hiding with Daimon behind a hydrangea bush, rushed us and plowed into me from behind.

"Aunt Ju-li-a!" she sing-songed, peeking at her aunt coquettishly from behind my blue jeans. I had prompted them in advance, knowing full well it was unlikely they would remember her. Surely she knew, but I didn't want to remind her of the fact. I wanted her to feel welcome, warm and surrounded by her loved ones. More than anything, I didn't want her to go away again.

"Samantha, you come here," she invited, dropping to one knee and holding out her arms. "And is that you Daimon?" He squealed with excitement, not because he remembered her, but because his sister was obviously delighted with this new relative. He got up his nerve to approach her and once done, felt immediately comfortable enough to start rolling his toy car up and down her arm. She hugged him and then ushered them into the living room with "Come see the tree."

"Tree? Home two days and your tree is already up? That's pretty fast, Sis."

"Yep. I couldn't wait to have a tree. It's been a long time, you know, and the house needed the scent of green."

"Well, this should do the trick," I said, admiring the fifteen-foot Douglas Fir, which looked surprisingly comfortable in its new abode, the ceilings easily accommodating its height. Against my better judgment, I scanned the tree for familiar ornaments. There were none. *She's not your mother.* Christmas was a full month away and Julia hadn't been back long enough to do any Christmas shopping, so there were no presents below the tree where I could discreetly place my gift to her.

Aware of my financial situation, she had been very clear about my not getting her anything this year. Still, with her being away for so long, I didn't feel comfortable showing up empty handed, so I copied an idea from some woman's magazine I found in the pediatrician's office. I needed to occupy myself while I waited for her and Paula to finish up in Malibu, so I picked the perfect orange, studded it completely in cloves (neat little rows, just like in the photo) and as instructed in the article, I attached a sweet bow at the top which was to serve as the hanger for this "lovely floral sachet for the closet." I wasn't sure where the 'floral' came in, but I had taken care to line up all the cloves just-so, and selected a lavender strip of thin satin for the top. I had managed to assemble the thing while babysitting the four neighborhood kids from down the street. I wrapped it in purple tissue paper with the lavender bow sticking out the top. Although it wasn't an expensive gift at least it was handmade. That always got extra points with Julia and I was sure she would appreciate it. For some reason my big sister seems to have a thing about her closet smelling good.

I couldn't very well slip it under the tree just to sit there by itself, and I didn't want to make a big deal of actually *presenting* it to her; after all, it was just an orange no matter how frilly it got. I was debating how to get it out of my coat pocket and into her hands without it seeming like a big deal, when she excused herself to go answer her phone. I took the opportunity to survey the area and check on my children.

The house, which had been closed up for the last two years, was in need of some sprucing up and Julia had hired a variety of people to get things back on track, including consultants to help her plan her upcoming nuptials. My hopes of a tranquil afternoon with my sister and the kids were dashed by the undercurrent of activity as big-city black-clad decorators conferred, cleaning ladies cleaned and repair people repaired. Samantha managed to corner two of the decorators, earnestly singing her heart out about a frog who hopped all the way to Hattiesburg. They smiled indulgently then tried to get back to business. "Wait, don't talk. There's more," she chastised.

Daimon was busy picking food off Paula's plate while her head was turned. *Well, at least he's quiet.* I can't help it, I find my children endlessly amusing, and adorable as all get out. So what if they wear other kid's hand-me-downs, these kids couldn't be any more precious.

Julia made the "I'm sorry" signal to me from the phone and pointed to what looked like a buffet table with a silver punch bowl in the center, set up for the workers and whomever else might happen by. I was hungry so I thought I'd pick a bit until she was free. I walked up the three steps to the "dining platform" not to be confused with the "piano platform"or the "fireplace rotunda." Naturally Julia would never call her fireplace room a rotunda, but others did.

Her home is a sprawling open-floor-plan of a house, with sections and areas on different levels, rather than actual rooms. It's all tiled with some modern version of Mexican pavers, inlaid randomly with marble and strategically overlaid with Persian rugs to help define the spaces. The entire west side of the house is glass: twenty-foot ceilings with floor-to-ceiling windows that frame a view of the town below. The furnishings are dark, highly-polished woods with light-colored casual cushions. The walls are cream colored and are a perfect backdrop for Julia's black-and-white photography which are artfully lit and tastefully flanked by the greenery of large tropical plants. Hand-blown glass sconces cast an amber glow over the main area of the house. The overall effect is somewhere between Mediterranean Modern and Casablanca. I know because that's how her house was described in the article that Art World ran about Julia's photography. I know most people are impressed when they first see it. They have to stop a moment to take it all in. But to me it's special because it's the house where my sister lives. It's a sanctuary she built from her imagination and paid for with her incredible talent and ability to understand what stirs the human heart. A reflection of Julia at her best.

I had long ago stopped comparing my lifestyle to my sister's. I had to, if I was going to maintain a good relationship with her, and that is something high on my list of priorities.

The punch bowl, a highly ornate silver basin, had been set out in the middle of the dining table and was surrounded by bite-size bits of fruit, cheese and little sandwiches. As I picked up the silver ladle my heart sank into my shoes. *Figures.* There, floating around in the beautiful punch bowl, bobbed several clove-studded oranges.

*Problem solved.* I dug out the gift from my coat pocket, unwrapped the purple paper I was sure she would have appreciated, and tossed it in to join its cousins. Well, she had said *no gifts.*

Somehow she managed to break away from the activity of the day and usher us all outside to play frisbee with the dogs. Paula joined us, but only physically, as she was busy catching up on paperwork from her perch on the upper deck above the pool. The children squealed until they almost choked, delighted with the silliness that Julia brought to the play. *How does she remember how to be a child, when she never had the opportunity to be one?*

* * *

**Later that evening** Paula boldly offered to babysit so Julia and I could get off together on our own. Not one to turn down free babysitting, I convinced my kids to cooperate and go with Auntie Paula to her house where they could play with a real-live talking bird. We drove out through the crisp, clear night, top down, bundled up and freezing our butts off even though the heater was cranked up full blast. I lay back counting stars while she drove. "Julia, sing me a song," I requested, feeling warmed by love, in spite of the cold. I gave myself over to the sensation of feeling like a pampered child as my big sister sang a song I remembered her singing to soothe me when I was young. "Oh, we ain't got a barrel of mon-ey, maybe we're ragged and fun-ny, but we're travellin' along, singing a song, side by side." I wanted to keep driving, heading west, into the sea and beyond to the other side, to the earth's end and right on up into heaven.

Too soon we reached Rancho Nicasio, a dinner/dance club not far over the county line. I had never heard of the place, but then again, I don't get out much. Her choice of restaurants surprised me. The minute we walked in the door I could tell we were a bit out of place. Most of the crowd was coupled and dressed in '40's attire. There was a good-sized dance floor around which the couples sat, sipping martinis and trying their best to keep in character. The band, called Swingtown, belted out tunes that had people leaving their entrees to get up and dance. We were seated in the rear and off to one side, Julia's choice, so that we could have some privacy, but the lively tunes kept us distracted and prevented us from getting into anything too heavy. I can read her like a book and I knew she'd decided to keep our first meeting since her disappearance light and fun.

I needed some cheering up and we needed to bond, what better way than on the dance floor? I couldn't make it through my appetizer without her pulling me up to dance. We had always danced well together, our basic sense of rhythm inherited from our mother. She twirled me until I was giddy, then taught me a new Latin rumba step she had picked up in Mexico.

Occasionally one of the few single men who clustered around the bar would pluck up his nerve and ask one of us to dance. She'd politely refuse, so I followed suit.

"You're not going to find a husband dancing with me all night. And who is this mystery fiancé anyway?"

"We'll have time to talk about that later, but for right now I want to hear about you. After all, you're my date tonight, Shelly," she said signaling the waiter. "Another Chardonnay for me please, and a Coors for my date," she informed the young man with the slicked back hair.

"You got it, sister," the waiter said, leaning in to give us a '40's-style wink.

"Why not order a bottle?"

"No, two's my limit, well maybe two-and-a-half, but that's it. I've discovered that if I drink too much I can't get anything done the next day, now that I'm a senior citizen."

"Senior citizen? You? Never. You still have more energy than I do."

"Well, I don't have two kids either."

"And you don't have Daryl."

"Thank God."

Julia paused, braced herself, then asked, "OK, what's the latest? Wait, I may need that whole bottle after all."

"What you might need is a very strong stomach. Daryl thinks he's going to be a porn star."

"A what?" She laughed so hard I thought she'd fall over.

"He got his hands on my last paycheck and before I knew it, he'd bought a camcorder."

"How did he ever get that idea in his head?"

"I think it was Laura and her french maid's outfit that got him started."

"Oh, please," she said shaking her head in disgust. "Who's Laura, and why is Daryl still living at the house?"

"Um, never mind about Laura, she's gone anyway. The truth of the matter, Julia, is that I can't afford to boot his ass out. I need him to watch the kids. I can't afford rent AND daycare—it's too expensive. The kicker to all this is I make too much money to qualify for any type of assistance. Now, if I were to quit my job and go on Welfare, I could make do." I watched her watch me stub out my fourth cigarette of the evening. "I know what you're thinking."

"What?"

"That I drink and smoke too much and if I were to stop smoking two packs a day at four dollars a pack . . ."

"They're that much?" she interrupted.

"Uh huh, then I could afford a sitter and . . ."

"I didn't say that."

"I saw the look."

"Well, maybe there's some truth in it. Maybe you could afford a few more . . ."

"What? Afford what? A sitter for two hours a day? Julia, you have no idea what it costs to be a single parent with two kids," I said, taking my frustration out on the cigarette butt.

"You're right about that. But I do know that there are ways to get what you need and want in this life. I know whereof I speak."

"Please, don't give me the 'I was so impoverished the only food I had was from sneaking apples off a neighbor's tree' speech."

"I wasn't. Gad, Shelly, you make me sound like a parent or something."

"Well, I guess you're entitled, seeing as how you're the closest thing I have to one." I leaned in closer, placing my hand on her arm. She stopped swirling her drink and looked at me, her eyes soft. "Julia, finances aside for the moment, I really do need your help. He bullies me into corners I don't have the strength to fight out of. I just fold up when he yells at me and I let him talk me into things that I know aren't good for me and the kids. I just can't get rid of him, he's like some pornographic tar baby. I really need your help, just one more time . . ."

"No, you don't."

"But . . ."

"You can take care of yourself, Shelly. You have the strength to break away from him and build a life for you and your children. I know you do."

"I'm afraid."

"I won't let him hurt you, you know that, but it's time you stop leaning on me. You can take control of this situation. You're stronger than you think."

"I'm not so sure. Sometimes the fear just wells up and paralyzes me."

"Don't I know it. But fear will rob you of your life."

"Easy for you to say. You've always been brave."

"Not always. I've spent my time in the dungeon, afraid to take the next step."

"What pulled you out? I feel like I've been in the dungeon my whole life."

"My desire to live in the light." I moved the food around on my plate, waiting for her to continue, to tell me something I could use. "There is so much beauty in the world, Shelly, so much harmony, you see it in nature everywhere. I consciously choose not to let the mundane rule my perceptions. I choose to trust life to show herself to me in all her sweetness. I choose not to wait until the moment of my death to appreciate this life experience."

"How do you do that?"

"Like I said, it's a choice. Even when things are hard, I wake up every morning and look for things to love about life, even if the only things I can find are small things, I start there and build on it. Even if it's just the color of the sky, even if it's the texture of this sweater, even if it's the fact that a rose has it's own unique perfume," she said, gently fingering a petal of the rose the restaurant had provided for our table. "There are things in this world, in this life, that are so beautiful, so perfect in their simplicity that they can pull us out of the muck and anchor us in the moment. That's where joy lives. I mean, right now, in this moment, the world for me is perfect because I love the scent of this candle and I love looking into your beautiful eyes."

My beautiful eyes began to moisten. "What about pain and disappointment? I know you've had your share."

"Pain? Well, I could turn my attention to the pain in my right knee, for example, but then I probably wouldn't feel much like dancing. And, my focus upon it would probably just make it worse. But, I know it's there, a reminder that the body has begun to give out little by little. A reminder that some day in the not too-distant future it will fail me for the last time. At some point, this body will scream at me and I'll be glad to leave it behind and just be who I really am—who we really are—pure spirit. And I, for one, do not wish to join my brothers and sisters in spirit, only to report back that I missed the beauty of life because I was so focused on the pain in my knee." She sat back, her gaze level. "Understand?"

"Julia, how do you come up with this stuff?"

"I didn't come up with anything. It's just how it is."

"It is what it is?"

"You got it!"

"So answer me this."

"Shoot."

"Are you going to visit Mom?"

"I guess so."

"What is it about your visit with her that you're going to love?"

## *Julia:*

She was smaller than I could have ever imagined. I watched through a space in the curtain as the nurse rolled her back over, whisking away the soiled pad beneath her. I could hear her whisper words of encouragement to my mother. The little bit of hair she had left stuck out randomly, white and spiky. The nurse smoothed it into place as best she could, and replaced the breathing tube that brought Mom oxygen from some unseen source. Once she felt certain she had made Nora as presentable as possible, the nurse showed me in, saying, "Isn't she just the sweetest woman?"

I smiled at the nurse without commenting as she drew back the curtain. Obviously Nora still had a way with strangers. "Hi Mom," I said moving to the side of her bed. She reached for a knitted cap to hide her baldness.

"Hello Julia," she said, presenting her cheek as if for the requisite good-night kiss. Dutifully, I kissed her. The butterfly-wing transparency of her skin softened my heart. I reached for her hand, but bumped her IV tube and decided to pat her shoulder instead. Her hand, skeletal and bruised blue-black from too many failed IV attempts, didn't seem to register the jolt. It had been twelve years since I had last seen her. Our last visit being hurtful enough to make me stay away, for good, or so I thought.

"Thank you for the piano," she said, referring to the gift I'd had delivered for her sixtieth birthday.

"You're very welcome," I replied. *Never mind that it's taken you more than a decade to respond.*

"How's Shelly? She hasn't been to see me, you know."

For some strange reason I started making apologies for my sister. "Well, Shelly's got the kids and . . ."

"My *grandchildren*, you mean! My *only* grandchildren whom I've never seen except in photos!" She began a coughing jag that lasted probably a minute, but seemed like ten, during which time I shifted back and forth from foot to foot, wondering if I should call the nurse. The coughing subsided finally, leaving her with a rather rosy glow, which I thought was an improvement over the pastey gray color her skin had become.

"Speaking of photos," I said, trying to be upbeat and change the tone of our visit, "I have some right here in my purse that I brought to show you." I took a seat, scooting the chair up next to her bed and began a tour of the limbs of her family tree. Although Shelly couldn't bring herself to visit, she was kind enough to have put together a little photo album of herself and the children at various stages of their young lives. On the cover of the album she had pasted letters made from bright construction paper that spelled out "For Grandma." Nora stared at the cover, her hands began to shake, and I felt like I was going to scream if she didn't open the album soon. Finally, she did.

I launched right in explaining the obvious to her, "This is Shelly pushing Daimon on a swing."

"Yes, Julia, I can see that. My eyes work just fine." She flipped the page. "This Samantha is a little cutie pie. Looks a little like her old grandma."

I leaned in closer so that I could see the photo, when I smelled a scent that I had never before detected emanating from my mother. She had always smelled like Juicy Fruit gum and Pall Malls to me. Her body odor now was one of cells breaking down and perishing one after the other. I pulled back from the unfamiliar odor, and came to Samantha's rescue. I didn't want Samantha to be anything like her grandmother. "Really, she's a dead ringer for Shelly, don't you think? Remember, Mom, when Shelly was that age?"

"Hmm, I suppose you're right."

Her cap had begun to slide off to the side and I reached up to adjust it, remembering her beautiful auburn hair and the starlet styles we'd try to copy.

"Don't," she said, jerking her head away. "Thank you, but I can do it myself," she said, trying to reposition the oversized cap. "Marilyn knitted it for me." Either Marilyn had overestimated the size of my mother's head or the chemo was shrinking her skull. I could see it would be a constant battle to keep it in place and I wished she could set her vanity aside and be at ease with her appearance in these last days.

Our first visit was short. Frankly, thirty minutes was all I could take, but I realized that *this was it* and if I was ever going to make peace with my mother, now was the time.

When I returned home I put my wedding plans on autopilot and devoted the next week to daily visits with Nora, which also meant daily visits with her oncologist, Dr. Jim DeLorzo, who made a point of keeping me posted on any change in her condition. Dr. Jim was a rather good-looking, silver-haired Italian with a trace of Tuscany in his deep voice. He was a serious fellow, but usually found a reason to smile whenever we'd meet. His smile reminded me of Turner's.

"The hospital staff is very disappointed in you and Shelly," Nora informed me one afternoon, the minute I arrived.

*Nice to see you too, Mom.* "And why is that, Mom?"

"The lack of visits . . . the lack of attention to your dying mother," she said between coughing fits.

"I'm here now, Mom."

"They're still disappointed, even Dr. DeLorzo." She said his name with an emphasis and a certain sideways glance that I knew was calculated to pull a reaction from me.

"He told you that?"

"In so many words."

Any time she said 'in so many words' she was lying. "I'll straighten it out with him," I responded in a purposefully nonchalant manner, as I assumed my customary position at her bedside.

"And what will you tell him?"

"I'll tell him we're doing the best we can."

"Hmpf."

"Hey, how about a foot rub?" I said swinging a brand new bottle of lotion in front of her like a metronome. "It's lavender-rose, and it's from Rosemary's Garden? Who could resist?"

"OK."

As I rubbed her feet, I remembered the matchbox bed I had made for her little toe when I was a child and wanted to keep her by my side. In those years I was under the impression that we would always love each other, would always be close. These were the feet that I had assumed would walk me through the trials and tribulations of my life, offering direction, an example to follow. I set aside the memories of abuse so that I could put as much love into my touch as possible. I massaged her feet to honor the woman she could have been, to honor the spirit form she would soon become. She began drifting off, humming a faint, familiar tune. When I was certain she was asleep, I finished the song for her, softy singing the words to the song I had always considered our song, "Side by Side."

At times it seemed as though her breathing stopped altogether, and as I held her foot—jiggling it until she half awoke and resumed a normal breathing pattern—I came face-to-face with emotions I had efficiently managed to hold at bay for years. How would I really feel once she finally leaves this world? Lost? Jubilant? Grown up? And what arrangements should I make for her remains? I had no idea whether or not she had made her wishes known. I needed to talk to Jim DeLorzo.

As luck would have it, he stepped onto my elevator as I was leaving and we rode down to the lobby together. We had no sooner greeted one another when I jumped right in, "Jim, when you have a moment, I'd like to discuss some particulars about my mother's prognosis."

"Certainly, how about now?"

"Now? Aren't you leaving for the day," I said, noting his white lab coat had been replaced with blue jeans and a work shirt.

"I am. It's Friday, three o'clock, my patients are being covered by Dr. Stewart, and I get to wear my other hat."

"It's not a Stetson, by any chance?" I said, noticing the boots—Tony Lama ropers.

He laughed. "No, Julia, I'm not a cowboy, just a weekend rancher. I do my best to herd grapes into wine."

"Not around here you don't," I said, making a sweeping gesture at the parking lot.

"No, I have a few acres in Petaluma."

"That's not far from me."

"Yes, I know. If you'd like, you can follow me up. I'm only about ten minutes off the freeway. We can enjoy a glass of my not-so-famous Merlot and talk about whatever is on your mind."

"I don't know, I wouldn't want you to take your work home with you. It might get confusing with all that hat switchin' goin' on."

He placed his hand firmly on my shoulder, "I don't get confused easily," he said, giving me a level stare. "And I'd like an opportunity to get to know you better, if that's alright with you." I tried to keep my shoulder as still as possible. "I understand this is not an ideal circumstance, but in the process of getting to know you, maybe I can help you sort things out with your mother. I can tell you have conflicting emotions where she is concerned."

"You are so right."

Jim's few acres turned out to be substantially more than a few. A small parcel by Texas standards, but in California wine country it was more than a modest estate. As for the Merlot, it was clear why he called it 'not-so-famous.' It was young and thin, not the most desirable attributes, at least not in a wine. You can tell a lot about a person by their home environment. It took me all of five minutes to understand that for Jim DeLorzo physical fitness is a way of life. There wasn't a room in his house that didn't scream: Exercise! Eat Right! From weight machines to magazines, it was all there. I never made it to his bedroom, but my imagination did a nice job of filling in the blanks. As far as I could tell, wine was his only indulgence.

A call from the hospital distracted him long enough for me to make a quick survey of his kitchen while looking for a water glass. No sugar would ever pass through these portals, nothing would ever be deep fried on this stove, and no Ben and Jerry's would ever come to rest in this freezer. Everything in his cupboards was either in labeled bags from the health food store or designated as organic and pesticide-free. One whole kitchen cupboard was given over to various supplements, most of which were foreign to me.

"It's obvious you're a proponent of clean living," I said, thumbing through a stack of Vegetarian Times. *I'm definitely back in California.*

"It's my work. In oncology you see time and again the effects of a system out of balance with nature."

"By system, I take it you mean your patients?"

"That's right. Poor diet, lack of exercise, nothing in moderation does take its toll." He was leaning back against the breakfast bar. *Was it my imagination or had he gotten taller and grown more hair since we left the hospital.* "For me it's not about living longer, Julia, it's about living better."

"That's my motto," I said taking a gulp of wine. "And then there are genetics to think about," I said, setting my glass down. I preferred whites, and this particular Merlot would give me a headache if I drank much more of it.

"Yes, and then there's that," he said. "Care to walk awhile?"

"Sure. Why not?"

"Julia, you barely sampled your wine. I warned you it's not that good."

"It'll round out a bit in time, I'm sure."

He laughed and slung his arm around my shoulder. "Can't fool you Sonoma girls when it comes to wine."

"Nope. Let's walk."

"Better put these on," he said, handing me a pair of rubber boots sitting by the door. "Just slip these on over your shoes, and you'll be fine, it can get a little muddy out there this time of year."

They were four sizes too large. "I feel like a duck in these things."

"Naw, you look cute, maybe even sexy."

"I doubt sexy."

"Hmm, you're right. But definitely cute. Ready?"

We walked for probably fifty miles, although he promised it was under two, and during that time I fed my senses on the unmistakable scent of Sonoma sage and the moist green rolling hills that had lured me back to this part of the world. I've probably seen more of the planet than most people, and I can definitely say beyond a doubt that, at least in my book, the Redwood Empire has it hands down over anywhere else. It is here that I feel expansive and most at peace. *How could I have lost sight of that over these last two years? From now on, if I'm bound to decorate apartments in my dreams, I'm going to make sure the apartments are in Sonoma County.*

During the course of our walk I was not surprised to learn that my mother was one of his Welfare cases. He believed in giving back to his community. In addition to his charity cases he volunteered one night a month at the Free Clinic. He also didn't believe in pulling punches. He informed me that my mother had somewhere between no time and three months to live, and that if I had any unfinished business with her it was time to get on with it. He was very matter-of-fact in this disclosure, correctly assuming I would receive the news objectively.

We walked in silence for awhile as I thought it over. He was giving me the perfect opportunity to unburden myself, but I decided to keep my internal struggles to myself for the time being. I didn't feel like dragging him into our family madhouse, and I didn't want to waste the moment, my first bit of leisure since returning home.

I did offer to pay his standard fee for her care, but he declined, saying "Let's just leave things as they are." I decided not to argue.

"You have a generous spirit, Doctor. I'm sure your patients adore you."

"Well . . ." he stammered, obviously uncomfortable with flattery.

"How do you see your role in patient care during their last days?" I asked, letting him wiggle off the hook.

"Good question. It varies depending on the emotional state of the patient and her family. Always I try to make the patient as comfortable as possible and I try, as best I can, to help her prepare for the inevitable. I don't believe in sugar coating the situation.

"Yes, I can see that."

"I believe people have a right to know just where they are on the wheel of life."

"How do you help your patients prepare?"

"That varies too, but generally I give them an opportunity to speak frankly about things they might feel uncomfortable telling family members. I listen. I try not to judge."

"You don't have therapy sessions with them, do you?"

"No, no, I'm not qualified. It's just that, in the end, about the only thing I can do for them is listen. So when I make rounds I sit with them and let them talk if they want to. You'd be surprised the confessions I hear. I doubt their priest knows some of the stories I'm told."

"And Nora? Has she told you anything you feel like repeating?"

"No, actually that's what bothers me about your mother."

"What do you mean?"

"She paints a picture of a closely-knit family," he said, glancing my way to see my reaction. I just kept walking, staring straight ahead, saying nothing. "She's especially proud of your achievements and the role she played in encouraging your talent."

I tried not to grimace. "And so why would that bother you?"

"I know she's lying."

* * *

By the time we reached the half-way mark in our walk, it was obvious to me that Jim DeLorzo was a very fit, sensitive, intelligent and caring man. It was also obvious that I was not as fit as I thought I was. I had to stop more than once to catch my breath when faced with even a moderate uphill climb. Also, by the time we reached the house it was clear that he's not the man for me.

How did I know? Although there was enough common ground between us to enable us to be friends, there wasn't enough spark to lead us into something more serious—not to mention, down the isle. It was my inner voice again. As certain as I was that Turner was the right guy, I was just as sure that Jim wasn't. Still I couldn't seem to let go of the idea that within less than a month I was going to be marrying *someone.* Why else would I continue full speed ahead with these wedding plans in spite of the odds? Especially when, in the eleventh hour, I'm turning my nose up at well-to-do, good looking doctors. The practical, Paula-part of my brain kept whispering *"Face it. You're nuts,"* while my gut kept urging me on. In that my gut has yet to steer me wrong, I decided to keep going down the path I was on, although I couldn't for the life of me see where it was leading.

On the drive home I tried to analyze my objection to this guy that most women would consider an absolute catch. I could put up with the bad wine, and I could get use to the long walks that had me wheezing by the time I reached his back door. I'm not so sure about living in a gymnasium, however, and it seems to me that one can carry the healthy lifestyle thing a bit too far. In the end, I couldn't come up with any real reason to throw back a perfectly good fish, but throw him back I did, although not before alerting my best friend.

"Paula, pick up, it's me."

"Hey, where are you? Shelly's been looking for you. She's already called here twice in the last hour."

"Something wrong?"

"I don't know. She didn't sound upset or anything. What's up?"

"Paula, I just spent the afternoon with your future husband."

"You what?"

"Put down your Diet Coke and have a seat. Do I have a guy for you."

Arranging a meeting for Jim and Paula was a cinch. I was barely in the door when he called to invite me to accompany him on a 10K run that weekend. I couldn't help but laugh.

"You don't expect me to actually run along side you, do you? You saw me huffing up that last hill to your house. You're joking, right?"

"Hmm," he said, I could sense him putting on his doctor's hat. "You might have exercise-induced asthma, we should check that out."

"Oh great, asthma! What's next?"

"No, I wasn't inviting you to run with me, but there is going to be a party afterward at the Yacht Club that should be a lot of fun. What do you think? It's for the American Cancer Society."

"A benefit run?"

"That's right."

"You know I think my friend, Paula, who is also a runner, was thinking about participating in that run." I could almost feel my nose begin to grow. "Would you mind if I brought her? She's a terrific runner and I'm sure the three of us will have a lot of fun together. She's my best friend," I added, to let him know how special I think she is. "I know you'll like her." Something in my tone must have alerted him to my intention.

He paused for a second longer than one would expect. "Great. No problem."

He's a smart man, perhaps he welcomed a set up. In any event, he took the bait.

"Can I meet you two at Crissie Field about half an hour prior, so we can warm up?"

"Sure," I said, volunteering away Paula's Saturday.

* * *

**"You told him I'm a terrific runner?!** Julia, you don't know that's true. You've never seen me run."

"Yes but, you run at the gym every day, same-same, right?"

"No, not same-same. But, I'm sure I can do a 10K, that's not the problem."

"OK, so what's the problem?"

"I don't particularly want to meet my future husband, as you like to call him, when I'm a sweaty mess."

"You look great when you sweat. Besides, your athletic prowess will melt his heart."

"You know, I'm beginning to wonder about what you are sure about these days. You're the girl who's sure she's getting married in a few weeks. We're getting down to the wire here, Julia."

"I know, I know, don't lecture. Will you come with me on Saturday? I've already committed you, so you are more-or-less obligated."

"This reminds me of that time in college when you told Jeffrey Banks I was an expert rock climber, never mind that I didn't know the first thing about the sport."

"Oh, I'd seen you climb over rocks before. I knew you could do it."

"I nearly killed myself!"

"Well, you didn't. And you'll do great in this 10K. Trust me on this one." I could hear her sigh on the other end of the phone. I know Paula, and I know that after the build up I gave Jim DeLorzso, she would have run 10K through hell to meet him.

* * *

As predicted, by the time Paula crossed the finish line she was a sweaty mess. I took heart in the fact that they crossed the line together and smiling. They made a handsome couple. I was waiting with two bottles of Calistoga and hearty congratulations.

"Well?" I asked, once we were in the ladies room and out of earshot.

"He's adorable!" she replied, so excited she practically bounced right out of her Reeboks. "Funny, smart, great legs. He had me laughing so hard I had to stop running and just double over!"

"See! Told you!"

"You were right! He's perfect!" she said, straightening her pony tail. "We're going to meet up tomorrow at the Farmer's Market to buy veggies. I'm surprised I haven't bumped into him there before; I go every Sunday, and so does he!"

"Great. Here, splash a little water on your face, you look flushed."

"Flushed? Probably so, but not from running. I tell you I could fall in love with that guy."

"I bet you could, and guess what?"

"What?"

"He's the first guy I've seen you get excited about that doesn't have some obvious defect for you to work on."

"Yeah? How about that."

"I'd say that's progress, Paula."

"Sure you don't want him?"

"Nope. He's all yours."

"That inner voice thing?"

"That's it."

"Well, your inner voice better come up with a guy pretty soon . . ."

"Lay off, Paula. Now, go get your man."

He was tall, easy to spot in a crowd. We found him drinking a sport drink with a female doctor friend of his from the hospital. As soon as he saw Paula he signaled her over saying "And here comes my buddy now!" It was obvious to both me and his friend, which one of us held his interest. "Julia, this girl can run!" he said, bragging about her perfect stride as he tucked her under one arm.

If it hadn't been for the fact that the two of them had manners, I would have felt a little left out. To their credit they throttled back on their enthusiasm for one another so that the three of us could make a tidy little circle of friends, chatting over our grilled eggplant sandwiches. I decided to let them have some time to themselves.

"Hey, what time is it?" I asked. "You know if I leave right now, I'll still have time to make it over to the WigWam on Chestnut before they close," I said, as if it was perfectly natural that I would have any interest in a wig store on a Saturday afternoon.

"WigWam? Never heard of it."

"Yeah, I found it the other day. It's right over here on Chestnut, next to Wells Fargo," I said, pointing off in some random direction. "Jim, could you do me a tremendous favor and give Paula a lift home? She lives about fifteen minutes from your place."

"Sure, I'd be happy to, but what's the WigWam and why are you in such a hurry to get there?"

"I'm going to buy a wig for my mother. If I hurry I can get it before they close. I'd like to take it to her today before visiting hours are over."

He put his hand on mine and looked into my eyes, "Julia, that's really sweet, but you know she'll be lucky to last the month. I saw her this morning, and it's not looking too good as of today. She's really taken a turn."

There it was, it had loomed on the horizon now for awhile, but I could feel in my bones that we had at last arrived. It was show time.

If I was going to have any truthful, real moments with her, it would have to be now.

"Well, there is one thing I know for sure about Nora," I said, patting his hand and smiling at Paula.

"What's that?"

"She'll want to die with hair on her head."

In my mind this was going to be the day we finally had a real mother-daughter, heart-to-heart, come-clean conversation, wherein she would finally admit to her abusive and reprehensible treatment of me and Shelly. I was prepared to forgive her, crawl in bed with her, wrap my arms around her and let her unburden herself. In short, I was prepared to help her die.

My expectations followed me in the door and waited impatiently at my side while she tried on her new wig. It didn't look as good on her as I had imagined it would. I had gone more for the color of it—a dark auburn—very close to the color of her hair in her youth. I had seriously misjudged the style. Her face was lost in the bouffant of curls.

"Well, let's see how I look!" she said optimistically.

I held my breath and handed her the mirror on her night stand.

"Oh!" she practically shouted when she saw her reflection.

*'Oh!?'* I thought I better get clarification on the exclamation before I launched into an apology about the style of the thing.

"Mom?" I noticed her eyes misting up as she stared, transfixed by her own image.

"Oh, it just takes me back. My beautiful curls," she said. Her fingers trembled as she adjusted a curl on her forehead.

*So it was a good 'Oh!' after all.* I sat down, relieved.

"Julia?" she began, grabbing for my hand as she collapsed back into the pillow. The sitting up and curl adjusting had worn her out. Not once in our visits had she grabbed for my hand. Her breathing was labored. It was going to be a serious moment, I could tell by the tone of her voice.

"Yes, Mom?" I said hopefully. Was this it? My mind reeled. Is this where she confesses her sins and asks for forgiveness? Is this the part where she says she realizes she's been a terrible mother, but that she had loved me anyway and she'd done the best she could under the circumstances?

"Yes, Mom?" I repeated, as a tear slid over her once prominent cheekbone and into her right ear. "Yes?" By that time, I was so hopeful and choked up by the sheer impact of what was taking place that I couldn't remain seated. I was on my feet, clutching her hand to my chest. I knew this was a difficult thing for her to do. I knew it was going to be hard for her to admit her failures, harder still to ask for forgiveness. But it had to be done.

All of us want to leave with as clean a slate as we can possibly muster. I was prepared to make it easy for her. I was prepared to forgive her. I was prepared to tell her a story I had heard recently and had been saving for just this moment. It was a story wherein a group of spirits, who all love each other very much, are preparing to incarnate again and are eagerly selecting the various roles they will assume for one another. 'And who wants to be my adoring father in this life?' one spirit would ask of the group. 'Oh me, me, I'll be your father,' and they'd all raise their hands. 'And who wants to be my best friend?' 'Here, I'll do it, let me.' They all volunteered to be a loving friend or relative to the one about to re-enter. Then someone asked, 'And who wants to be the one who causes me pain?' 'Not me!' 'Count me out.' 'I think I'm busy that week,' they'd reply, none wanting to be the one to cause pain. 'But how else will I get my lessons? How will I grow?' the spirit asked. Finally a particularly bright spirit stepped forth from the back of the crowd. 'I'll be the one. I'll take on that role, regardless of the karma it will create in balance for me—for I am the one who loves you best.'

Somehow in my desire to forgive her I had allowed myself the luxury of believing that, from a spiritual perspective, she had loved me enough to take on karma on my behalf, in order that I could grow. I needed to heal my life and I had given Nora the power to do it for me.

The tears slid down her cheeks, her chest heaved with repressed sobs, "Julia?" she managed to croak once again.

I clutched her hand and sobbed with the poignancy of the moment. Her lower lip quivered, then she said, "Have you ever been to Atlanta?"

"Atlanta?! Atlanta! You're asking me about Atlanta at a time like this?"

"Yes, Atlanta. Atlanta, where Scarlett O'Hara lived," she said innocently.

"You're lying here dying and all you can think to say to me is 'Have you ever been to Atlanta?' I gave her back her hand and marched out of the room. *That's it, I'm never coming back.* I knew I was going to have to compose myself before I got in my car. I walked down the hall to the elevator and rode it down two floors. I thought of Shelly and how hard she struggles to make sense of life. I thought of what Nora's life could have been and what she had let it become. I thought of the mother I had desperately loved as a child, and I thought of the countless random beatings and the psychological hell she had put us through.

After hitting the side of the elevator with my fist a few times, I rode it back up. I had at last come to the realization that she would die in denial of the hurt she had caused my sister and me. My anger was fueled as I thought of the difficulties Shelly had in overcoming the effects of her childhood. As far as I was concerned, her poor choices in life were a direct result of her lack of self worth. A nice little legacy, courtesy of our mother.

When I reached her room she was looking at herself in the mirror again, probably imagining herself still a dead-ringer for Scarlett.

"Put that mirror down and look at your daughter," I demanded. Expressionless and reluctantly she complied.

"I have a favor to ask." I paused long enough to calm my racing heart and relax my balled-up fists. This was it. The culmination of all our years together was coming down to this one moment in time. I knew I had to get it right. I knew that what I said to her now would either free me or forever haunt me. Silently I vowed that these would be the last words I ever spoke to her. I looked her directly in the eye, as my energy filled the room. I was about to make a request, but in fact I was issuing an order, and I had to stand firm in my power.

"Mother, if there is any way you can arrange it, I would appreciate not encountering your spirit again." She didn't respond, but I held her gaze, nonetheless. I took a deep breath and continued. "Nora, if you have a choice, please choose not to know me."

"What?" she said, finally realizing what I was requesting. "That's a fine finale to our visit."

"No, Mom. Make no mistake. This is a finale to our relationship, in this and any future lifetimes. I don't ever want to know you again, under any circumstances."

* * *

**I never found out** what she thought of all that, if anything. She was saved by the bell. Her phone rang, and without another glance or word to me, as I turned to walk out of her room, she began a chatty conversation with someone who had dialed the wrong number.

I should have known better. With all my years of being *directed* and my great faith in trusting my inner guidance, I should have known. No one person will ever love us exactly the way we want to be loved. The simple reason for this is that no one will ever really know us. We all have secret recesses where others are denied access. We even hide from ourselves when we think we need to. The only exception is that grander, wiser part of ourselves, that eternal self that gently guides us through the maze of the life we've chosen. We do have access to the perfect love we seek. And seek we do. And seek, and seek, and seek. When really all we have to do to find the one who loves us best, is be still.

She died a week later. She died alone. Shelly had to fight the urge to beat herself up over not visiting her when she had the chance. After the cremation I kept the ashes where people commonly keep such things, on my mantle, until I could figure out what to do with them. There are rules about where one can and cannot scatter, a fact unknown to me but made perfectly clear by the crematorium representative. Not that it mattered much, who was to know? I'd put her where I pleased once I knew for sure where the best place would be.

Once Shelly fully accepted the fact she was gone, it was like someone had taken a heavy suit of armor off her. She looked like she had suddenly dropped fifteen pounds.

As for me, the darkest hour had been that day I left her hospital room. I drove out to the coast to walk barefoot in the cold, wet sand for hours, shouting into the wind the things I would have said to her if I had stayed longer. The following week, when Jim phoned to say that she had passed on, I felt very little. Certainly not remorse, I had moved past that. I just hoped she remembered my admonition at her bedside.

A few days after she died the dreams began, random snippets from my past all lining up like coins waiting to fall neatly into a slot. And every night a recurrent image would visit me. I'd dream about my mom smiling and flying overhead in a white dressing gown with her auburn hair streaming down her back. She'd never say a word, just smile and wave good-bye over and over again. I wasn't sure how it all pieced together, but I was sure of one thing: I needed another session with my therapist.

## *Paula:*

"I haven't received a bill from you yet," she said into the receiver in a sing-song voice. It was meant to be a mild chastisement.

"And you won't either," I sing-songed right back at her.

"Paula, you promised."

"I lied. Guilty. I flat out lied. I knew you'd never agree to our sessions unless you thought you were compensating me."

"Now I feel awkward, knowing you were just doing me a favor."

"I can do you favors if I choose. Besides, you're getting married and there is nothing too big for the bride to ask of her best friend." I had given up on the idea of knocking some sense into her, and wisely so, as it was only serving to piss her off. Now I was just going along with this fantasy of hers, getting swept up in the momentum of the wedding, like good friends should. Besides, I reasoned, knowing Julia the way I do, I wouldn't be surprised if the perfect man dropped from the sky and landed next to her at the altar.

"Well alright, but the truth is, I need another session."

This was not what I had expected. *Another session?* "Another session?"

"Yes, please. How does your schedule look for tomorrow? I'll understand if you don't have time, but I thought I'd like to get in one last session before the wedding."

"Tomorrow? No, no tomorrow's fine."

"You've helped me so much already, and I thought that if I could clear up this one last thing . . ."

"Two o'clock fine with you? My last appointment tomorrow is scheduled to end at one, then I can grab a bite and meet you in my office at two. How does that sound?"

"Like a done deal. Thanks, Paula."

"Don't mention it. Besides it's the least I can do to repay you for sending Mr. Wonderful my way."

"I'm glad things are working out for you two."

"You knew they would."

* * *

My appointment preceding Julia's was with Felicia Welton. I was eager to see her. My replacement reported that she had not kept her appointments after the assault. Even though I had been back for a while, this was the first I'd heard from her. She had ignored the numerous calls from my secretary trying to schedule her.

To my utter amazement, the heretofore immaculately groomed and coifed sophisticate strolled into my office wearing jeans and tennis shoes. Her hair was pulled back into a pony tail. There was something different about her face too, I thought. I studied her as inconspicuously as possible while she settled herself in the recliner. No, I decided it wasn't her makeup. Her makeup, aside from being a little toned down, was pretty much unchanged. She was wearing serenity, that was the difference.

"Hello, Felicia. You look well."

"I feel great," she said, straight on, eye-to-eye, no squirming. I could tell she wasn't kidding.

The story came out in our session. Soon after her hospital stay, Felicia's husband had a stroke. With his right side paralyzed, the all powerful Charles Welton was forced to come to terms with his own frailty. Once they realized he didn't have the mental edge he once had, the Weltons sold off their various enterprises and shifted gears. Slowly Charles came to accept the fact that he was reliant on Felicia to tend to his daily physical needs, which were numerous. Felicia accepted her new role and tackled it admirably.

"What about hiring a nurse?" I asked, once it was clear that her days and nights were being consumed by her nursing duties.

"I don't mind, really. I prefer to do it myself. We have a physical therapist that comes once a day to help Charles with his exercises, but otherwise, I've found that I rather like caring for my husband. Not only is he showing an astounding amount of bravery in dealing with his infirmity, but he's always taken such good care of me over the years and it feels good to be able to return the favor." She looked wistful, happy even.

I got busy taking notes. "And have you had any sexual 'adventures' lately?" I asked, using her preferred terminology for her infidelities.

"Oh heavens no!" she laughed with a dismissive wave of her hand. "Those days are long gone."

"How's that?"

"It's funny, now that I have Charles all to myself, I find I really have no need of anyone else."

"And your sexual needs? How are you handling that?"

"Oddly they seem to have diminished. What Charles and I share now is much more fulfilling than any casual fling I've had in the past. Our sex life isn't exactly what it once was, but we share a greater intimacy now than ever before. Once Charles realized he needs me to perform the most mundane of tasks, I think he came to understand he needs me emotionally as well. He's become very reflective since the stroke," she said, gazing out the window. "I fully expected him to be morose, and imagined him passing his days glued to the television watching CNN or some other business-related commentary. I've discovered that his interests are a lot broader than I assumed. I've discovered that his interests include me."

She reached for a tissue before continuing. Although she wasn't crying, she still needed a moment to compose herself. "Certainly our life style has changed. Those we considered friends seem to have other things to do these days and we've not been invited to functions like before." She cupped her hand to the side of her mouth, as if to share a secret, "It seems we're off the 'A list' now," she said with a half chuckle. "For the most part, it's just the two of us and we seem to have re-discovered what it was that so fascinated us about the other in the first place. It's odd that it would take something like this to put our marriage back on track."

"Have you been able to share your past with him, Felicia?"

"Yes. I wasn't sure about the timing, but I decided that if we were to make a clean start, I'd have to reveal myself, warts and all."

"How did he take it?"

"He cried. Then we cried together and held each other for about a day."

"I'm proud of you," I couldn't resist saying.

"I'm proud of us, Charles and I, we share everything now." She leaned forward in her chair, her face clear and open, "Isn't that what women really want in a relationship?"

Julia arrived early, as I suspected she might. She looked eager, determined, very matter-of-fact. She was wearing a white cashmere turtleneck, cream-colored wool slacks with a camel blazer. Her hair was pulled back in a broad tortoise-shell clip. Around her neck was a metal medallion.

We embraced and she seated herself in the recliner. She did not, however, recline. Instead she sat on the edge of the chair, very straight and business-like. *She's always had good posture.* There was no small talk; she was prepared to get started. I wondered what she had in mind.

She slipped the medallion off and handed it to me. It was heavy, about the size of a sand dollar and looked like a sunburst. In the center was a figure of a woman holding a ball of light. The inscription that ran around the rim was in Latin. Try as I might, I couldn't quite get the translation.

"It means something along the lines of seek joy—all else will follow," she offered. "Maybe not that exactly, but that's the general idea."

"Where did you get it?" I asked, feeling its weight.

"It was my mother's. She wore it all the time when I was a little girl, even slept in it."

She flinched slightly, perhaps remembering something painful. "I use to beg her to let me wear it."

"Was there some point in time when she stopped wearing it?" I asked, following a hunch.

"I don't remember seeing it after about age five."

"Isn't that about the time she married Tom, your stepfather?"

"Yes, that's right. I didn't see it again until I was in my twenties. I had forgotten about it, and then . . ." she stopped abruptly, trying to capture a memory.

"Go on," I prompted, but she was silent, staring off into some distant past. I waited while the clock clicked off the minutes. "Does this carry a special significance for you?" I asked gently, turning it over in my hand—the back side was blank.

"It does. This is difficult for me." She stared down at her lap and picked at her sweater. "You remember that foolish incident, that suicide attempt back in my twenties?"

"Of course I remember," I said, "I almost disowned my brother over that one." I sat up on the edge of my chair, like she was doing: two ramrods on a mission.

"I was unconscious for three days," she said blushing. "It was a serious attempt. I've never spoken to anyone about that episode. I've been quiet about it because what I experienced was very personal, very private. But now, if you're going to help me, you need to know."

I sat completely still and silent, respecting her pace.

"While I was unconsciousness, I spent some time outside my body, on some other plane. Paula, I'm pretty sure I spent some time on the other side," she said, more serious than I had seen her in a long time.

"You believe you had a near-death experience?"

"Perhaps."

"Do you remember any tunnels of light, anything along those lines?"

"No tunnels, but I remember a beautiful light and swirls of color like how it must seem on the inside of a giant soap bubble."

Somehow I could imagine it. "Anything else?"

"Right before I came to, I saw a hand reach down from above and present me with this medallion."

"Literally? Is that how you found this again?" When it came to Julia I had always believed anything was possible.

"No, not literally, but it might as well have been, it was so real." She rose and walked over to the window. The filtered light patterned her face in a way that I had seen before and I found myself thinking how beautiful she is, such a bright flame of a woman. "And then I heard a voice," she continued.

"What did it say? Was it male or female? Loud or soft?" I asked, busily jotting down notes to review later.

"I couldn't discern a gender, but it was a commanding voice—both strong and gentle at the same time. 'Take this and remember who you are' is what it said."

"Boy," I said fingering the medallion. "So then what? Did you tell your mother? Did you ask her for it?"

"I did. She said she hadn't seen it in years, didn't know where it was. So that was that. I tried to talk myself into believing it was just a dream." She walked back over to the recliner and had a seat, only this time she sat back, relaxed. "That is until the other day, when it was given back to me."

"I'm listening."

"After I left my mother's bedside, having admonished her never to darken my door again, I was pretty shook up. I could barely believe that I had said that to a dying woman, to my own mother. A part of me was feeling a little guilty, while another part was feeling vindicated and powerful."

"That's natural, Julia, after what you'd been through with her."

"Paula, all she had to do was admit she was wrong and apologize. I was all set to forgive her and reclaim her, as it were, but she never gave me the chance. It was beyond her to do so and I could see that finally."

"So what you said to her, was that to punish her?"

"Not at all. It was to free myself. When she died, I spent some time with Shelly trying to help her sort out her feelings. When I examined my own, I was relieved to find that I felt pretty neutral about her death. That is until I walked back into her house. Remember when I went down to Pacifica to dispose of her possessions?"

"Yes, of course I remember. If it had been me I would have put it off until after the wedding. I was amazed you did it when you did."

"It was better that I took care of it right away. Shelly had no interest in any of Mom's belongings, nor could she walk back into that house under any circumstance. Because I was feeling so neutral about the situation, I thought it would be easy."

"How did it go?"

"I was fine until I walked into her bedroom. Her scent was still there. Her old scent, before the cancer. That's the one thing I've always loved about her. The room smelled like that part of my mother that I've somehow managed to love, in spite of everything else. It's the scent I remember from childhood, when I was very young and my mother was everything to me." She inhaled deeply to allow her olfactory senses their memory. "So, I just broke down and cried those tears that were waiting off in the wings somewhere; those tears I had in reserve and didn't expect. After I was cried out, I decided to take a shower and then spend the rest of the night hunting around for old photos or anything else I thought we might someday want, before I called the Goodwill to come and haul everything off."

"That's when you found it? During the hunt for the photos?"

"No, that's not how it was at all. Mind you I hadn't stepped foot in that house for over twelve years, but of course I remembered where the towels are kept. I opened the linen closet to get a clean towel. They must have all been in the laundry because there was only one in the closet and it was at the bottom of a stack of sheets. I lifted the sheets and pulled on the towel. Underneath the only clean towel in that entire house was this medallion," she said, holding out her hand toward the medallion I had held onto during her tale.

"Of course, I knew it was meant for me. When I held it, the voice I had heard when I was unconscious, came rushing back to me."

I handed her back her treasure. "And now how do you feel?"

"Well, there's more." I nodded for her to continue.

"Since her death, I've been having dreams where she's whole again, hovering above me, looking happy. I notice her hair is back to normal and she's wearing a white robe."

"Does she speak?"

"No, she just waves good-bye until she fades away or sort of floats off."

"Is it always the same?"

"Well, it was, until the last time I had the dream?"

"You stopped having it?"

"Yes. The last time, as she was disappearing into a mist, the hand with the medallion appeared again, just like before."

"Were there any words this time."

"No. But I've never forgotten what was said before, so there was no need. It was just a reminder."

"A reminder of what?"

"A reminder of who I really am."

"And that is . . . ?"

She leaned back in the chair, closed her eyes, and said, "I'm spirit, having a human experience, just like you, just like Shelly, just like all of us. And because I'm spirit evolving I choose my experiences, every one. I chose that my early years would be traumatic. And I've chosen to experience loss as part of my growth, as part of learning to let go. For all the lessons I've created for myself and have experienced, I am grateful. But there is one part of the human experience that is harder than all the rest."

"What part is that?"

"Our dual nature. We are spirit, but we are human too, with all the emotions and frailties of human nature. So now, I've come to ask you to help me find a way to forgive her. Paula, I need your help."

I left my chair and walked to hers. I wrapped my arms around her and whispered in her ear, "You've got that, my friend."

"There's one more thing," she said looking up at me.

"What?"

"I want to feel good about wearing this," she said, as she brought the medallion to her heart.

We agreed there is no time like the present. I decided that because EMDR had worked so well for her last time, we'd use it again. Before we started, however, I felt there were a few things that needed to be cleared up.

"Often victims of abuse . . ."

"Wait, Paula," she said holding up her hand to interrupt me, "I've never seen myself as a victim. If anything, I see Nora as the victim."

"How so?"

"When she was a young woman she had great beauty and talent. She had dreams and aspirations. But what she didn't have was the strength to stay whole in the face of a tyrant. She was not true to herself, so she lost herself and became victimized in the process. After a while she didn't remember any other way to be and her life became habit. Then she lost more. She lost her self respect and later her children. She lost pieces of herself to cancer. You know, many years ago when she first contracted cancer, she never told me. She never told me she'd had a radical mastectomy."

"Really?"

"Nope, not a word. I was her opponent, by that time."

"Had been since around puberty I would imagine."

"That's right. I guess for her to admit to me that she had lost a breast was to be defeated yet again."

I nodded. My friend had come to me trusting I could help her. As she put it, she wanted to *feel clean* when she said her vows in a few days. She reminded me that I know her better than anyone. She reminded me of the great confidence she has in me.

I excused myself a moment to retrieve us both some water, to stretch a minute, to do what Julia had always suggested I do when in a situation where I need strength: I asked for guidance. I'm not sure if guidance is what I got, but as I stilled my mind, an idea did come to me. When I returned to my office I knew I had hit upon the right approach.

I suggested that she was in conflict about forgiving her mother. Not only because of the abuse she sustained, but because when one throws the blanket of forgiveness over the wounds of the past, everything goes, the baby with the bath water, so to speak. What Julia wanted, was not to wad her childhood up into one compact lump that she could file away in her forgiveness file and never access again. She needed some memory she could retrieve that would allow her to feel that at least at some point in her life, her mother had loved her. Then she could forgive.

We went to work. As I mentioned before, Julia is a person who can visualize extraordinarily well and is therefore a good candidate for Eye Movement Desensitization Reprogramming. We worked for hours on diffusing and discharging the more prominent wounds from her childhood. When I asked her if she needed a break, she kept her eyes closed and replied that she wanted to push on. It wasn't until close to six o'clock that I finally thought she was ready. I chose to communicate directly to her higher self, and as I moved my hand back and forth rhythmically before her eyes, I asked that Julia be provided with an image she could keep and return to—one to represent the love she and her mother had once shared.

From this prompting, Julia's subconscious offered a picture that pleased her. She saw herself as a child, lying in the crook of her mother's arm, fingering the medallion that lay upon her mother's chest, while Nora spelled out *I love Julia* in the night sky with the coal of her cigarette. I asked her to bring the image into sharp focus by infusing it with other sensory information. She made the picture more real by visualizing little Julia breathing in her mother's scent, while she listened to a faint tune in the background that had, at one time, been their song.

"Now what shall we do with this memory?" I asked.

She suggested that we wrap it in a giant colorful soap bubble and send it drifting off toward the heavens. And so we did. We created a place where it would always be safe and easily retrieved by Julia whenever she pleased. Whether or not Nora had ever written those words in the night sky is anyone's guess. It's hard to remember that sort of thing from childhood. Sometimes a memory just needs a little assist.

## *Shelly:*

Up until that moment, I felt as though I'd lived my life in parenthesis. Suddenly there were exclamation marks everywhere: Run! Get out! Hurry! Take this! Leave that! Stay calm! If the fish were biting, I had another hour or two. If not, he could be home any minute.

I had been secretly packing for weeks and storing the boxes next door at Sue's. I was careful to make it look as if nothing was being removed. Sue had contributed some miscellaneous kitchen items, odds and ends, that I was going to need. Best of all, she had contributed her support and her truck, which the two of us had packed to the gills once we were sure the coast was clear.

The TV, sofa, double bed, a dresser and three kitchen chairs were all the furniture we could manage to take and still have room for the boxes. There wasn't that much room in the new place anyway. It didn't matter. I had seen Julia's very first apartment and I knew that with the right combination of cinder blocks, plywood and sawhorses I'd be able to put together any missing items of furniture. We'd make do. We had to.

Thankfully, Julia had been able to take the children for the afternoon. I didn't want them to see their home being dismantled, to feel this energy, to sense my fear. I decided that when I picked them up and brought them to their new home, I'd make it like a big surprise. *Look kids, here we are at our new home!* I just hoped I could think of something to say when they asked where's my swing set? Where's Daddy?

I had decided to keep my sister in the dark about what I was doing until I had actually done it. It was time I stood up for myself. For the first time in my life I was taking a major step forward without eliciting her help. Although I did plan on taking her up on her offer to pay my attorney's fees for the divorce, the rest I was doing on my own. She was right about one thing—I do feel better about myself since Mom's death. Sometimes, I feel so light, I practically float right out of my skin.

We were right on schedule. Three fifteen and the truck was loaded. I gave Sue the thumbs up that she had been watching for in her rear view mirror. Without a backwards glance, she peeled out of the driveway, toppling over one of the kitchen chairs that hadn't been tied down. We hadn't taken the time to tie down anything. Sue was a total bundle of nerves over this thing. She was just sure Daryl would blame her for being an accessory to the *get-away* and then find a way to take his anger out on her. I knew he wouldn't, but I agreed to the plan anyway.

Last Friday when Daryl was home, she'd come over for a visit and staged an argument with me, solely for his benefit. I told her I didn't think it was necessary to go that far, to which she said, 'I don't want him looking in my direction when he realizes his TV and kids are missing. Yes, as far as I'm concerned, it's necessary. In case you hadn't noticed, he's one scarey dude.' Somehow or another we had pulled it off—our imagined quarrel—without breaking up laughing. Daryl witnessed her slamming out of the house, screaming something to the tune of, I'm never speaking to you again!

"What was that all about," he had asked.

"Don't ask. The bitch!" I had replied. He shrugged and returned to his beer and the wrestling match on TV without another thought. I phoned her later that evening, when he went out for more beer, to tell her our plan had worked. We both did our own private version of a little victory dance.

Standing on the front porch for the last time, I felt a little sad. Sad that we hadn't been able to do better by the children. There was no pretense of love any longer. The truth was, I had gotten pregnant with Samantha and had caved in to his insistence that we get married. I hardly knew the guy. I've had a lot of regrets since then, but my children are not one of them. I said a silent thank you for my kids and prayed for strength, before I turned my back on what I had come to accept as my life, my reality.

I'm not sure where I got the moxie to leave. The County housing subsidy had finally come in, making it financially possible, and the fact that Julia was home and once again available helped too. I didn't have time to stop and figure it out right then, but I caught my reflection in the window as I turned to leave and thought, *Maybe I've just had enough.* Whatever the reason, I vowed as I shut my car door, that once this day was behind me, I wouldn't be afraid any more. A brave declaration for someone whose hand shook as she placed the key in the ignition. The car started right up like it was anxious to leave. The engine raced and so did my heart. I pulled away from the curb anyway.

The guest list was short, the preparations lavish and the groom still unaccounted for. I had shared my frustration with Paula. She had suggested that I stop badgering Julia about this supposed wedding and just let her play it out however she wanted to. She was determined to go ahead with this, and if Julia was determined, there wasn't a thing that could alter her course. Still I had to admit to having a little problem with her going ahead with a wedding when I didn't know who was going to be my future brother-in-law. When anyone asked who's the lucky guy, she'd just smile and say 'You'll just have to wait and see.' If I was around, I'd mouth behind her back, 'She doesn't know.'

I wasn't surprised by the drama that surrounded the event. She's a Leo, after all, and had grown up in L.A. in the fifties with a wannabe starlet for a mother. Drama just naturally followed. The week before the wedding she had hired an assistant who did nothing much more than field telephone calls. Everyone was curious about Julia and her fiancé. Julia's assistant had a script that covered the inquiries but left the caller scratching her head. She confirmed the wedding was still on, gave directions to the site, and reminded the guests to dress warmly. Other than that they'd have to wait until the wedding to satisfy their curiosity.

Finally the day arrived. The small cove of a beach that she had chosen for the ceremony had been transformed. Against the back of the cliff face, three white party tents had been erected and firmly anchored. The large one in the center faced out to the ocean, while the two smaller tents on either side formed a semi-circle which provided sheltered seating for the guests. The flowers were abundant, as was the food and beverage. Every detail had been carefully thought out and faithfully executed. This was to be—in her words—her last wedding, and she wanted it to be perfect.

She had taken care of the problem of the cold weather by strategic placement of twelve towering mushroom heaters, the heat from which was efficiently captured by the tents, making the evening quite comfortable. Further out on the beach was a rather large bonfire, attended by two women dressed in white toga-style gowns. Fortunately, the day had been mild, only a bit overcast and the tide tables confirmed that our feet wouldn't get wet during the ceremony.

The guests were mostly female. The exception being Dr. Jim, who escorted Paula, a few male spouses accompanying their wives, and one big surprise: Patrick, Paula's big brother from L.A. Without Paula being aware of his arrival, Patrick had shown up early enough in the afternoon to help the crew set up.

To personally greet each guest as they arrived, Julia stood with her feet in the sand at the bottom of the ramp leading down to the beach. She looked ethereal. Aside from the beaded combs that held the hair back from her face, she wore her hair lose and scattered with wild flowers which were held in place by hair glue. I had no idea there was such a thing as hair glue, but for Julia's sake I'm glad she knew about it, otherwise her look wouldn't have held up to the sea breeze. Her face was scrubbed clean, without a trace of makeup. Over a white body suit that she wore for warmth, flowed an iridescent ivory sand-length garment. It was studded with prismatic beading and tucked strategically to skim her body gracefully. She wore no jewelry and was barefoot.

Ethereal or not, when Paula saw her brother, she thought Julia had some explaining to do. I didn't want to miss her reaction, so I scooted on over by Julia.

"Julia, what is Patrick doing here? You didn't tell me he was coming, and why is he dressed in white? Isn't this a bit odd?"

"Let's see, question number one: he's here because he's going to be involved in the ceremony. Question two: I wanted to surprise you. Question three: Patrick being dressed in white is strictly a coincidence. I told him he could dress however he liked."

"He's going to be in the ceremony?" Paula asked, her voice rising involuntarily.

"That's right," Julia responded, cool as a cucumber. "Paula, Jim, here are your seats, right up here in front," she said to a stunned Paula. She lead them into the main tent, through the flaps which were draped in netting and held back by twisted garlands of plumeria, irises and orchids. Julia's favorite flowers.

Paula didn't know what to expect, but she wasn't ready to give up hope that some mystery groom was hiding in the wings and kept craning her head around whenever a male guest arrived. Anyone would do at this point, anyone besides Patrick.

I sat up front with Samantha and Daimon, right across from Paula and Jim. It was a treat to see Paula so flustered. Julia's right, that girl sure can worry. And Julia was determined to prove Paula's worrying useless. I was pleased to notice that in spite of Paula's agitated state of mind, her boyfriend had a soothing effect on her. He put his arm around her in a protective, tender way that made my heart leap. I wondered if I'd ever find someone to feel that way about me.

I wasn't convinced, however, that if I found a man to care for me, he'd add anything substantial to my life. With my steady job, my new home and Samantha and Daimon to love, my life was in better shape than it had been in a long time. My divorce was underway and Daryl, rather than coming after me like I had feared, showed up at work the day after I left him to inform me that as far as he was concerned I could have anything left at the house—he was moving in with his latest girlfriend. So after all the worry and planning, it turned out alright. I guess things do have a way of working out.

The music, provided by a string quartet, began to play something well-suited to the occasion. It was no "Here Comes the Bride," but it was a beautiful piece that sounded like something you'd find in the New Age/Classical section at Back Door Records. It was then that Julia began her walk down the aisle, alone and empty handed, but absolutely radiant—just like every other bride.

Once she reached the front, she turned and addressed her friends:

"Thank you for coming to my wedding. This summer a Mexican woman, whose prescience I respect, told me I would be married by the end of this year. As you can see, this is about as end of the year as you can get." The group chuckled, and Julia continued. "I told her that I didn't want to get married, and I meant it. Still, I held myself open to the possibility that the fates had something special in store for me. I hoped for someone who would love me unconditionally, someone who would make me whole and set me free. A tall order, I know. With such an event looming on the horizon, I looked very carefully and extra hard at my life. In the process of preparation for this event I asked my dear friend, Paula Knapp, to help me get my house in order. Along the way, I met that person."

She turned to the side and beckoned to someone standing off to her left, hidden from view by a draped area.

"Patrick, would you join me, please?"

I could see Paula stiffen. For a minute I thought she was going to pass out. Patrick came forward to stand at Julia's side, and the two of them stood facing the crowd, holding hands and beaming. They made a picture-perfect couple.

Patrick opened a small notebook he took from his pocket and looked out into the crowd. He smiled at his sister. "As an ordained minister of the Church of Light, I have the authority to perform this ceremony. Some of you may recall that in the sixties anyone of us could send in one dollar and become ordained ministers in this and other similar churches. That is exactly what I did some thirty-odd years ago. I tell you this because although this ceremony is not considered a traditional marriage and I am not your typical minister, I can assure you that the vows taken this evening, by our friend, Julia, have been well considered and are binding by nature of their sincerity and intent. Furthermore, they are binding by the power invested in me as a minister of the church, according to the laws of the great State of California."

With that, he turned toward her and they faced one another. I could see that Paula had started breathing again.

"Julia, do you understand that these vows which you are about to take, before your friends and family, are sacred?"

"I do," she replied.

"Then place your right hand over your heart and repeat after me, if you will, these words: I, Julia La Chance, do solemnly swear to love, honor and cherish that part of myself I know to be my higher self."

She repeated his words. I was surprised to learn she had switched back to her maiden name and I wondered what other surprises she might have up her sleeve.

"And do you, before God and this assembly, further agree to the following. If so, you will please signify by stating I will." She nodded, and he began:

"Do you swear that you will live your life in accordance with your inner knowing, regardless of the expectations of others?"

"I will," she stated.

"And to that end, do you promise to make a daily practice of stilling mind and body to better listen to your higher self?"

"I will."

"Do you promise to walk gently upon this earth in awe of God's wonders, acknowledging that you and all of God's creatures are an individual spark and expression of the Divine?"

"I will."

"Do you further agree to live by your word, considering promises to self as important as promises made to others?"

"I will."

"Do you promise to resist the temptation of the ego, which include any manner of word or deed that is intended to put you above another?"

"I will."

"Do you promise to remove yourself from the temptation of judgment of yourself and others, trusting that life unfolds in its own perfection and time."

"I will . . . promise to try."

*That's my Sis,* I thought, shaking my head, knowing her tendency to over-analyze, even at the most inappropriate times.

"Do you also promise to remember at all times that you are spirit, having a human experience?"

"I will."

"And finally, and to that end, do you promise to dance like no one is watching?"

To this, she laughed and said, "I will."

And true to her word, she did, later that evening around the bonfire and at the water's edge with her friends. After a few glasses of champagne, Paula commented to Jim that Julia looked like some Druid goddess at beltane. She was so relieved that Julia and Patrick wouldn't be sharing a honeymoon suite, she wasn't making much sense.

At times I just had to sit back, cuddle my two children and watch her, radiant and vital, moving through the crowd. No one knows better than I, my sister's secret fears and the balancing act she performs to keep her life from splintering. I know where she's been, and how far she's come. And that knowledge gives me hope.

* * *

Everyone agreed it was one of the best weddings they had ever attended, and one that would surely last. The festivities lasted longer than anyone expected, but we were all having such a good time that we stayed until the stroke of midnight and then some. I suspect that because of my sister's ceremony, the New Year's resolutions that were vowed that night were a bit different than the usual promises of calorie counting and gym attendance. I know mine was.

Earlier that day, Julia and I scattered our mother's ashes in the ocean at the water's edge in the very spot where Julia now, in the glow of the bonfire, lifts her skirts and twirls and twirls. I guess it stands to reason that Mom might be watching. I don't know.

Oh, I almost forgot. In concluding the service, Patrick hung some sort of medallion around her neck and pronouncing her whole unto herself, turned her around to face her friends, saying simply:

"Ladies and Gentlemen, I present to you, Ms. Julia La Chance."

That's when the music started.

# Reading Group Questions and Topics for Discussion

1. Throughout *The Reluctant Bride*, Julia is alternately portrayed as practical or mystical; powerful or frail; complex or natural; disillusioned or hopeful. What does her chameleon-like nature say about her? In what ways does her inability to define herself enhance her life? In what ways does it dis-empower her?

2. When Julia is informed of her upcoming marriage, one of the first things she does is write a page in her journal about the desperate emptiness she and Shelly experienced in childhood. In what ways does Julia's marriage atone for her childhood?

3. Julia turns to her protégé, Paula, to help her sort through a painful past. How did this request affect Paula and her friendship with Julia? Was it calculated on Julia's part? Have there been times in your life when the balance in a friendship was upended? What was the outcome?

4. Do you believe Julia is truly guided by the cosmos or is it something she imagines in an attempt to feel loved and cared for? Have you ever felt directed or guided from On High?

Thinking back, have there been times of synchronicity in your life which you ignored and wished you hadn't?

5. Julia apartment shops in her dreams. What relevance does this have to the central theme of the book? Discuss what feelings are evoked by the word *home*.

6. Discuss the importance of identity. How do the main characters define themselves?

7. Did Julia allow herself to be controlled by Turner? Was the relationship detrimental or instrumental to her growth?

8. Marriage brings many things to the women in this novel. Did Julia really believe she would find her soul mate and marry by the end of the year? Is Julia truly reluctant to marry? How is her marriage in the final chapter a metaphor? What does it represent to Julia? To Shelly? To Paula?

9. The men in this novel are peripheral characters. Nonetheless, their influence reverberates throughout the lives of the main characters. Discuss the nature of Turner, Lucky, Tom, Patrick and Daryl. In what ways are they similar? Why do you think the author created these male characters this way?

10. Nora's life is forever changed in the scene where Tom destroys her piano. Why is this so? In what way does this ultimately impact her daughters?

11. When Julia arrives to rescue Shelly from Nora, Shelly refuses to go. Discuss Shelly's character. Is she driven by loyalty? Fear? Is she jealous of Julia?

12. Discuss Julia's behavior in her final visit to her mother. Was she heartless or justified?

13. Was the sprinkling of Nora's ashes the day of the wedding an attempt to include Nora or was it symbolic of final closure?

14. What does the book's ending imply about Julia's, Shelly's, and Paula's future? Do you think any of them have been transformed over the course of the book? If so, how?

# About the Author

C. K. Veale is a chiropractic physician and the founder of the Women of Power Manifesting Workshops. She is a member of the International Women's Writing Guild and Left Coast Writers.

She lives in Sonoma County, California.

www.ingramcontent.com/pod-product-compliance
Lightning Source LLC
Chambersburg PA
CBHW030251290526
45785CB00001B/50
* 9 7 8 1 4 1 0 7 0 0 6 7 4 *